For Andrea—
    a love story

Granville Burgess

Dusky Sally

357 W 20th St., NY NY 10011
212 627-1055

DUSKY SALLY

First printing: July 1987
ISBN: 0-88145-053-7

Cover art may be reproduced only by permission of Broadway Play Publishing, Inc.
Design by Marie Donovan
Set in Aster by L&F Technical Composition, Lakeland, FL
Printed on acid-free paper and bound by BookCrafters, Inc., Chelsea, MI

About the Author

Granville Burgess received an M.F.A. in directing from The Catholic University of America. Currently he is Creative Director at The Westbeth Theatre Centre in New York City, where he helps oversee the American Playwright Program and directs productions of new plays.

Dusky Sally won the following awards for Mr. Burgess: Honorable Mention, the 1985 CBS/FDG New Plays Program; Winner, Circuit Theatre Mid-South Playwrights Competition; Winner, Dayton Playhouse Playwriting Competition; and Winner, The Drama League of New York New Play Contest.

Mr. Burgess's next theatrical project is the book for a musical, *Conrack*, which will open at the AMAS Repertory Theatre in New York in September 1987. In addition to authoring plays, his television writing credits include two children's musicals, "Paul Revere Rides Again" and "Common Sense," the soap opera "Capitol," and an episode for "Tales from the Darkside."

The recipient of grants from The National Endowment for the Humanities, The U.S. Department of the Interior, The Redskin Foundation, Theatre-in-the-Works, and International Humanities, Mr. Burgess also was awarded writing fellowships at The Edward F. Albee Foundation and The Millay Colony for the Arts. He recently completed an artist-in-residency at Central State University in Oklahoma, teaching playwriting. His play *The Freak*, about the psychic Edgar Cayce, appeared Off-Broadway at the Douglas Fairbanks Theater during the Spring 1982 season.

Mr. Burgess currently is writing a screenplay for a film about his childhood in Greenville, South Carolina.

ACKNOWLEDGMENTS

Every play I write is influenced by people too numerous to name. For better or worse, I am willing to let any intelligent being—and sometimes some not so intelligent—throw in his or her two cents worth. There are, however, those who must be cited for their special contributions to *Dusky Sally*. I could write pages on how much their generous gifts of time and energy have meant to me, but I hope mere mention of their names will suffice.

Any list must begin with my siblings, Mary Wyche, Caroline, Frank, and Vicki; my wife, Andrea; and my parents, Mary and Alfred, who together bear the first brunt of my desperate gropings for Truth and Beauty. After them, in totally random order but truly grateful appreciation, are: Stephen Zuckerman, Michele Shay, Arthur Kopit, Jack Chandler, John Sedlak, Allen Coulter, Ted Bent, Rob Meiksins, Tommy Gower, John Bishop, Dee Wedemeyer, Maria Nelson, Sheldon Epps, Wayne Adams, Marty Markinson, Brent Peek, Joe Treen, Peter Orton, Paul Latchaw, Helen Merrill, Bill Craver, Bruce Bouchard, Peter Clough, Jennifer Greenfield, The Capitol Rep Cast, and the Playwright's Lab at Circle Rep.

NOTES ON THE PRODUCTION

The play should be a seamless, continuous whole. The stage never goes to black. Characters flow from one scene to another without interruption. When furniture is to be moved, it should be done by the actors themselves, if possible. If stagehands are necessary, they should change the scenery behind or even around the actors while the scene is commencing. The play should have a "concept" design that emphasizes costumes and lighting as the real "scenery", as much as possible. Whatever the design, the play should never, ever stop moving forward.

The two acts should look and feel very different. Act One is light and airy, full of color, and, for the most part, gay music. The costumes, even the servants', reflect the incredible wealth and liveliness of Paris before the Revolution. Act Two, by contrast, is heavier in tone, drab and earthy in color, reflecting the harsh realities of life on a plantation in 19th-century America.

The play is full of music and song, both within scenes and as transition from scene to scene: in Paris, harpsichord and orchestral sounds; in Monticello, slave songs. In some scenes, environmental sounds are used as transition music. Whatever the instruments or voices, music is a crucial element in the production.

Finally, an acting style should be employed that matches the heightened level of the language, a style more in keeping with the epic plays of Shakespeare than with today's modern realism.

INTRODUCTION

"How about a play about Sally Hemings?", my
friend answered when I asked, only half in jest, for a
subject for my next play.

"Who?"

"You know, Thomas Jefferson's slave mistress."

There followed the proverbial jaw-drop. No, I did
not know—and I had majored in American history.
No, I did not know—and Thomas Jefferson was my
favorite American. No, I did not know—but I was
about to find out!

Five years later herein is printed some of what I
learned—with the emphasis on the "some." I read
books about France during the Revolution, plantation life in America, social histories, political
histories, narratives of slaves, anthologies of black
folklore, biographies of Lafayette and Madison—
and, of course, anything and everything I could find
about my two central characters.

Jefferson was easy. He himself kept meticulous
records on everything from the dozens of varieties of
peas he planted to the precise day when each flower
on his plantation first blossomed. Slave births,
deaths, and runaways; crop yields; daily tempera-
tures—the man was obsessed with recording his life.
He even invented a machine to simultaneously copy
letters as he was writing them—and he wrote hundreds and hundreds of letters. Historians, having
poured over these records and many, many more,
have written voluminously about this fascinating
man. And yet, when I had read my fill, I had to agree
with the standard aphorism about the man: Thomas
Jefferson is our most written-about American, and
our least understood. He recorded the outer facts of
his life, but seldom the inner feelings. He remains, as
the historian Merrill Peterson described him, "an

impenetrable man." So at least I would not be called to task for not having written *the* Thomas Jefferson, because there isn't one!

But what of Sally Hemings, my title character? Interestingly, there is practically nothing at all in the historical record about her. We know she was the daughter of Elizabeth Hemings, a slave, and John Wayles, Jefferson's father-in-law. We know she went to France as maid to one of Jefferson's daughters. We know she and Jefferson were the subject of a newspaper exposé published during his presidency. Her son and another Monticello slave gave newspaper accounts in Ohio in the 1870's affirming the relationship and stating that Sally Hemings bore several children by Jefferson, the first being conceived in Paris. The Jefferson heirs hotly deny that any relationship existed whatsoever—see Virginius Dabney's *The Jefferson Scandals* for a point-by-point rebuttal of the allegations. Other historians have unearthed some intriguing facts to prove that it did—Fawn M. Brodie, in her *Thomas Jefferson: An Intimate History*, proves that the family denial—which states that Sally's children were fathered by Jefferson's nephew, Peter Carr—is simply not true, because Carr was definitely not at Monticello nine months before all of these births, whereas Thomas Jefferson denfinitely was. As I write this, *The New York Times* has been publishing a running debate in its Letters column between scholars and lay people rehashing the whole argument yet again.

Where does all this leave the dramatist? Fortunately, with a controversial topic! But also with a heavy responsibility not to sensationalize for the sake of selling tickets. I am, after all, dealing with a great man here—and a great woman, I might add—and I take that responsibility seriously. So when the historian in me waged war with the dramatist on the Field of Truth, who won the day?

Not surprisingly, the dramatist. Not that I took the historical record lightly. I clearly remember trying to place the opening scenes of Act II in precisely the month and year that Sally would have been pregnant and Jefferson at Monticello. Or worrying whether I could cause James to appear in an Act II scene after he was in fact historically dead. Or agonizing for months over a decision to have Jefferson say to Sally something emotionally revealing that he had in fact said to someone else. But in the final analysis I had to agree with Aristotle that poetry is a higher art than history. In order to reveal greater truths I had to sometimes sacrifice lesser ones. It was enough for me to know that Sally Hemings did exist, and that there is information in the historical record to admit the possibility that she was Jefferson's lover. I did not, as I've said, write of this relationship cavalierly, but I did, ultimately, do it with the conviction that my job was not to report or record, but to create. *Dusky Sally* is my creation, and I take full responsibility for its characters and their actions.

Some will quarrel with this approach. Many, no doubt, will be angry that this play was ever written. A friend who teaches at the University of Virginia told me that, in a highly complimentary one-man show about Jefferson, when the name Sally Hemings was merely mentioned several audience members left the theatre. Some theatre professionals refuse to see this play as anything but a historical drama with no relevance to today. And I shall never forget a man in Albany who called in while I was on a talk show and excoriated me for writing "lies" about America's greatest statesman-philosopher. He said it was "appalling" to suggest that Thomas Jefferson had ever had a relationship with a black woman.

I answered that the fact he found it "appalling" was precisely why I had written the play. What is it, I asked him, that makes it so repulsive to think that this great white man and this lowly black woman quite possibly could have loved each other? Why do we Americans, 200-plus years after Thomas Jefferson wrote the words, find it so impossible to believe that, indeed, all men are created equal? Why are blacks excluded from living in Forsythe County, Georgia, or are beaten and chased in Howard Beach, New York? Why does television report the rise of racism on college campuses? And why is America still struggling to fulfill the promise of freedom and equality for all its citizens that our Founding Fathers made for us so many years ago? Alas, Jefferson might still be speaking to us today when he wrote, "I tremble for my country when I reflect that God is just, and his justice cannot sleep forever."

I take Thomas Jefferson to task in this play, but it was not my intent to diminish him. I know too well how hard it is to translate ideals into actions, and I am even more convinced that he was one of the greatest men ever to grace this planet. I was trying to humanize the man and, hopefully, show that there is a little bit of him in us, and a little bit of us in him. And I like to think that, were he alive today, he would not only forgive my casting a spotlight on his feet of clay, but would actually applaud my humble effort to make the inspiring words of his famous Declaration reverberate once more.

As for Sally Hemings, I salute her as one of the truly great enigmas of our times—and a wonderful joy to create!

GRANVILLE BURGESS
New York City
Memorial Day, 1987

If poetry is the little myth we make,
history is the big myth we live, and,
in our living, constantly re-make.

Robert Penn Warren

Dusky Sally was originally produced as the winner of the Mid-South Playwrights Competition at Circuit Playhouse in Memphis, Tennessee, Jackie Nichols, Executive Producer. It also was produced under the title *Master Jefferson's Mistress* as winner of the Dayton Playhouse Playwriting Competition, Jim Payne, Managing Director.

Dusky Sally received its professional premiere at the Capital Repertory Company, Bruce Bouchard and Peter H. Clough, Co-Producing Directors, Robert Meiksins, Literary Manager. It was directed by Jack Chandler, assisted by Jennifer Greenfield. The Set Design was by Jack Chandler, assisted by Wade Battley; Lighting, by Jane Reisman; Costumes by Randy Barcelo; Sound, by Andrew G. Luft and Crispin Catricala; and Movement by Constance Valis Hill. The Production Stage Manager was Patrician Frey, with the following cast, in order of appearance:

JAMES HEMINGS .... L. Peter Callender
THOMAS JEFFERSON .... Pirie MacDonald
MARQUIS DE LAFAYETTE ... Richard Maynard
PATSY JEFFERSON .... Katherine Leask
SALLY HEMINGS .... Erica Gimpel
JAMES MADISON .... Richard Maynard

CHARACTERS
(*In order of appearance*)

JAMES HEMINGS*—Playful, humorous, mocking outside, burning with intense anger and hatred inside. Born 1767.

THOMAS JEFFERSON—Tall, red-haired, intellectual, ambitious, in control of himself and all around him. Born April 13, 1743.

MARQUIS DE LAFAYETTE—Bold, witty, charming, soldierly, very French. Born September 6, 1757.

PATSY JEFFERSON—Tall, plain, reverential, possessive. Born September 27, 1772.

SALLY HEMINGS—Extremely beautiful mulatto, intelligent, direct, earthy, loving. Born 1771.

JAMES MADISON**—Cautious, conservative, shy, always dressed in black, with a large conical hat. Born March 16, 1751.

---

*The actor playing JAMES also plays the slave in the final scene. He should be unrecognizable as JAMES.

**It is possible for the part of MADISON to be played by the actor playing LAFAYETTE.

Act One

Act Two

ACT ONE

Scene 1

(The Drawing Room. Paris. Afternoon, late summer, 1787. In the dark we hear singing.)

JAMES:
When you walk-a that lonesome Valley
You got tuh walk it by yo'sef;
No one heah may walk it with you,
You got tuh walk it by yo'sef.
You got tuh live a life of service,
You got tuh live it by yo'sef;

(The lights come up to reveal JAMES *on his knees with a measuring stick.* JEFFERSON *stands over him.)*

No one heah to live it faw you,
You got tuh live it by yo'sef.

*(*JEFFERSON *takes two large steps.* JAMES *measures them.)*

JEFFERSON: How much?

JAMES: Six feet.

JEFFERSON: Again.

(He again takes two large steps. JAMES *measures them.)*

JAMES: Six feet, Massuh.

JEFFERSON: Just what I thought.

(He goes to his desk and begins doing calculations on a piece of paper. JAMES *gets up and goes to the telescope and looks out.* JEFFERSON *continues figuring.)*

JEFFERSON: That's not what I told you to do.

JAMES: Yessuh.

(JAMES *begins dusting the books.*)

JEFFERSON: No one could be more anxious to see that carriage than I. But the time will pass more quickly if we're occupied, you with your work, I with mine.

(*Master and slave go about their separate tasks for a while.* JAMES *hurriedly completes his and leaves the room. As soon as* JAMES *is gone,* JEFFERSON *goes to the telescope and anxiously looks out. Nothing. He looks at a thermometer outside his window and records the temperature in a small notebook.*)

JEFFERSON: August 13 . . . Ninety-eight degrees . . .

(JAMES *enters with the* MARQUIS DE LAFAYETTE *close on his heels.*)

JAMES: The Marquis de Lafayette.

JEFFERSON: Not another step. Did you walk?

LAFAYETTE: And suffer the importunings of a thousand beggars? If the king doesn't act soon, 1787 will be the end of the Bourbon monarchy. Besides, it's too hot to walk.

(*He hands his hat and gloves to* JAMES, *who retires to a corner of the room, seemingly occupied with his work, but actually, as always, listening intently to every word.*)

JEFFERSON: You must exercise, my friend. Today I walked from the Board of Trade on Boulevard Ste. Marie to my home. 1,535 doublesteps in thirty-five minutes, at approximately three miles per hour.

LAFAYETTE: How do you know?

JEFFERSON: (*In a verbal flurry*) My doublestep is exactly six feet. There are 5,280 feet in an English mile, or 880 Jefferson doublesteps. Dividing the thirty-five minutes into the 1,535 doublesteps gives approximately 44 doublesteps per minute—or three miles per hour.

LAFAYETTE: I am sorry I asked. But let me tell you why I have come.

JEFFERSON: I flattered myself it was because I sent for you.

LAFAYETTE: Please, Thomas, leave flattery to the French. We invented it and are the people most supremely qualified to use it!

JEFFERSON: I see what you mean.

LAFAYETTE: You are pleased to joke with me. But to more serious matters. I have read your *Notes on Virginia*. (*He holds up a small book.*)

JEFFERSON: And?

LAFAYETTE: You must never publish it, Thomas. If you do, history will not treat you kindly.

JEFFERSON: History is merely a set of agreed-upon lies, according to your Monsieur Voltaire.

LAFAYETTE: I am serious, Thomas. Your opinions disturb me greatly.

JEFFERSON: (*Surprised*) On what? On Virginia's rivers, her agriculture, her different religions—

LAFAYETTE: On her black people. How can you, of all people, hold such base opinions?

JEFFERSON: (*Exploding a little.*) Base opinions?! What do you—

(JEFFERSON *catches sight of* JAMES, *who immediately ducks his head and resumes working.*)

JEFFERSON: James, go outside and watch for your mistress. I wish to know the minute she arrives.

LAFAYETTE: (*With genuine affection*) Jimmy, have you learned yet to cook my *escargots à la bourguignonne*?

JAMES: *Avec beaucoup d'ail.*

LAFAYETTE: Bon!

JEFFERSON: (*Paternally*) James is becoming an excellent chef, aren't you, James?

JAMES: Yessuh, Massuh. An' I'm mighty grateful to you for gettin' me taught.

JEFFERSON: Run along now.

(JAMES *exits.* JEFFERSON *speaks forcefully.*)

JEFFERSON: What do you know of Negroes, sir? I have lived among them my whole life and what I wrote I based solely on scientific observation.

LAFAYETTE: But surely all Negroes do not fit your descriptions?

JEFFERSON: There are exceptions of course. But science deals only with the norm.

LAFAYETTE: Promise me one thing: You will consider revising your *Notes on Virginia*. Further "observation" may change your mind.

JEFFERSON: If it does, I shall. Believe me, my friend, no person living wishes more sincerely than I do to see the refutation of the doubts I have expressed about these people.

LAFAYETTE: *Bon.* (*Withdraws his snuffbox.*) Snuff?

JEFFERSON: No, thank you. I shall never understand the fascination of inhaling a powder directly into your brain.

Lafayette: The exhilaration of exhaling it directly out of your ears. But I confess, it was chiefly to show you my new box.

(JEFFERSON *looks at the snuffbox.*)

JEFFERSON: Good lord!

LAFAYETTE: Have you ever seen such an exquisite *derrière*?

JEFFERSON: I am amazed, after looking at that, how you manage to find your nose.

LAFAYETTE: You should try it, Thomas. It makes one feel *très passionnant.*

JEFFERSON: Being "très passionnant" no longer holds the same fascination for me. Now to my business. As Ambassador to France, my instructions from Congress are to shift some of our trade from England to France. But your Comte de Vergennes is a crafty negotiator. I need your help in persuading him—

(JAMES *bursts into the room, followed by* PATSY *and* SALLY.)

JAMES: She's here! An' guess who's come with her!

PATSY: Papa!

JEFFERSON: Patsy, dearest. (*They embrace. With real tenderness:*) Daughter, it's so good to have you with me again. How you've grown!

PATSY: Yes, I'll soon be as tall as you. I know, I'm not to worry: It gives me "stature." But look at you. If Mama could see you now.

JEFFERSON: In Paris the only thing more tyrannical than the King is fashion. (*He hands her a present.*)

PATSY: For me?

JEFFERSON: With the love of a doting father.

(*She opens it. It is a ring.*)

PATSY: Oh, Papa, it's beautiful! (*She puts it on.*) Thank you! (*She gives* JEFFERSON *a hug.*)

LAFAYETTE: And it is made even more beautiful by she who wears it.

JEFFERSON: Oh, forgive me, my friend. Patsy, I want you to meet the Marquis de Lafayette.

LAFAYETTE: (*Kissing her hand, and with great flourish.*) *Enchanté, Mademoiselle. Marie, Joseph, Paul, Yves, Roch, Gilbert du Motier à votre service.*

PATSY: (*With a terrible accent*) *Merci, Monsieur. C'est un honeur de rencontre le liberateur des Americains.*

(LAFAYETTE *winces.*)

PATSY: Didn't I say it right?

JEFFERSON: Perfectly. But, I fear when a foreigner speaks French, it produces a kind of national earache in native Frenchmen.

LAFAYETTE: Ah, I see you have brought a friend. (*Taking* SALLY'S *hand to kiss it, and again doing his "routine".*) *Enchanté, Mademoiselle. Marie, Joseph, Paul, Yves—*

(SALLY *withdraws her hand.*)

LAFAYETTE: *Qu'est-ce qu'il-y-a?*

JEFFERSON: And who is this?

PATSY: It's Sally, Papa. Don't you remember?

JEFFERSON: Sally Hemings?

SALLY: (*Meekly*) Yes, Master.

JEFFERSON: My instructions were to send someone older. (*To* SALLY) Why didn't your mama send your sister?

SALLY: Critta took sick at the last minute. But I'll work hard for you, Master, you'll see.

JEFFERSON: I don't know—

JAMES: I'll look after her.

JEFFERSON: Hmmm.

PATSY: Don't send her back, Papa. She's my age, and a good maid. When I was seasick, Sally mixed a potion that completely soothed me. Let me keep her, Papa. I like her. Please?

JEFFERSON: I can refuse you nothing. (*To* SALLY) But at the least sign of trouble—

SALLY: I won't be no trouble. Thank you, Master.

JEFFERSON: (*To* LAFAYETTE) You'll stay to dine, of course. James has cooked your favorite.

LAFAYETTE: *Avec plaisir.*

JEFFERSON: Go along now, daughter. How I've missed you. We'll never be separated again.

PATSY: Promise?

JEFFERSON: Promise.

PATSY: (*Hugging* JEFFERSON.) I love you, Papa.

JEFFERSON: And I, you.

(PATSY, JAMES, *and* SALLY *exit.*)

LAFAYETTE: What an exotic creature, this Sally.

JEFFERSON: Yes, the deplorable result of our slave society's more boisterous passions.

LAFAYETTE: Thomas, you cannot keep slaves in France.

JEFFERSON: I shall pay her a salary, as I do her brother.

LAFAYETTE: And if they discover that in France they are legally free?

JEFFERSON: Then we shall see what they want to do. Do you expect me to turn this child loose in Paris?

LAFAYETTE: Jimmy is not a child.

JEFFERSON: And "Jimmy" is learning to be an excellent cook. So that when he is emancipated there is at least some hope he will be able to make his way in the world. My friend, if politics has taught me anything, it is that an unsuccessful effort at emancipation, attempted too early, will only rivet still closer the chains of bondage. We must await a more propitious time.

LAFAYETTE: Beware the seduction of human bondage, Thomas. You may find that the time is never propitious.

JEFFERSON: Do you think I enjoy owning slaves? Never could I see how any rational being could propose happiness for himself from the exercise of power over others. And I swear to you, when an occasion occurs in which I can interpose with decisive effect, I shall know, and do my duty with promptitude and zeal. Now, please, no more unpleasant thoughts to mar my happy day.

(JEFFERSON *and* LAFAYETTE *exit. Beat. Then* JAMES *steals into the room, crosses to* JEFFERSON'S *desk, and picks up* LAFAYETTE'S Notes on Virginia. *As he sits in* JEFFERSON'S *desk chair and begins reading, the lights change to . . .)*

Scene 2

(*The Drawing Room, six weeks later, early morning.* SALLY, *carrying a pitcher and a towel, slowly enters. Awed and frightened by her strange surroundings, she attempts a weak hum to steady her feelings. When* JAMES *senses her presence inside the doorway, he stuffs* Notes on Virginia *into his pocket and turns to greet her.*)

JAMES: Nice room, idn' it? Yessir, the French like to do everything with style! (*Imitating French dandies.*) "*Voulez-vous vous asseoir, Monsieur?*" "*Merci.*"

(*He sits very grandly, remains dignified a moment, then sprawls all over the chair.* SALLY *does not respond.*)

JAMES: Used to be I could make you laugh with my "mockin' ways." Pour that water in the bowl.

(JAMES *gets a foot bowl from a shelf.* SALLY *spills the water.*)

JAMES: I said the *bowl!* You tryin' to make more work for us?

SALLY: I'm sorry, James, I just . . .

JAMES: You scared, Rabbit?

(SALLY *nods.*)

JAMES: What of?

SALLY: Everything. This language, this house, bein' sick . . .

JAMES: You just had a reaction to the inoculation. Same thing happened to me.

SALLY: Why did he do that . . . that . . .?

JAMES: Vaccination.

SALLY: An' then lock me away for so long? Five whole weeks!

JAMES: So's you wouldn't infect other folks. Gotta protect his property!

SALLY: He had it, too, didn't he? He rolled up his sleeve an' showed me the mark, so I wouldn't be afraid. Said I'd always have it, just like his. (*She examines her mark.*)

JAMES: We bear enough of his marks.

SALLY: I had such dreams, James. I was back at Monticello, in our special place in the nook of that ol' oak, lookin' out across the mountains. 'Member how we used to look at that sky full of white clouds an' pretend one of 'em was gonna turn into the hand of Jesus, scoop us up, an' carry us over the mountains to Canada? Drop us in a field of flowers! Only this time, when I was floatin' over the mountains you weren't with me an' I looked back at Monticello an' Mama was there playin' with her hair the way she does when she's tryin' not to cry an' I could even see Master in his bedroom lookin' after me through his telescope—I could actually see down it into his deep blue eye—an' I started cryin' out, "I don't wanna go! Take me back, Jesus, I wanna go back!"

JAMES: You got to stop dreamin' so much, Sally. Now you know Mama musta had her reasons for sendin' you. Critta didn' really take sick, did she?

SALLY: No. Mama said I had to be the one. Said Critta was too old, too beat down already. What'd she mean, James?

JAMES: Mama knows the longer you suck in slavery, the more you cain't spit it out. There comes a time when you been bent down so long, you don't know how to walk straight. You don't even *wanna* walk straight no more. That's the day you got to look out for, the day when Satan's done snatched you to his bosom! Slavery's easy, Rabbit. Freedom's what's hard.

(SALLY *is frightened.* JAMES *holds her.*)

JAMES: Oh, sister, it's a sign you've come, I know it. There's something in the air here, Sally. Folks is riled up, an' I'm gonna find out why. Ol' man Jefferson got me tutored in French so's I'd be a proper chef, but that don't mean all I got to talk about is food! (*Excited*) Listen, Rabbit. There's a gatherin' in the Place Ste. Germain tonight an' I'm goin'!

SALLY: You mean sneak out?

JAMES: Yeah, it's time. An' when I think you're ready, you're comin' with me.

SALLY: What if the master finds out?

JAMES: He won't care. We're special, Sally, you know that. Master Wayles fathered his white babies in the day an' visited Mama at night. So ol' Tom won't do nothin'—why, we're practically kin! (*He laughs ironically.*)

SALLY: I'm scared, James.

JAMES: Rabbit! You remember our promise to Mama, don't you? "Ain't no struggle more supreme,"—

SALLY: "Freedom is the onliest dream."

JAMES: Right. Now come here an' give me one of Mama's mashes. I know she musta sent one with you.

(SALLY *hugs* JAMES *hard.*)

JAMES: "Mama, stop, you're mashin' me!"

(*They laugh.*)

SALLY: You know what I missed most, James? My birthday present.

JAMES: Aw, Rabbit, I cain't do that no more. I'm too old.

SALLY: You better never get too old for my birthday present, James Hemings. An' I want it now.

JAMES: But it ain't your birthday.

SALLY: You got to catch up first. I'm ready.

JAMES: I'll do it for you tonight.

SALLY: The Tar Baby can sit right here.

(*She moves* JAMES *into place.*)

JAMES: Sally—

(SALLY *covers her ears.*)

JAMES: Sally!

(*Resigned to his fate,* JAMES *begins reciting the Tar Baby story, with* SALLY *playing Brer Rabbit and* JAMES *the Tar Baby. They act out the whole story in great detail. It is an ancient ritual with them.*)

JAMES: Well, Brer Fox went to wuk one day wid some tar an' some turkentime an' fixed him up a contrapshun what he called a Tar-Baby to catch Brer Rabbit, an' he set it in de road an' lay off in de bushes fer to see what de news wuz gwineter be. Sho nuf, bymeby here come Brer Rabbit—

SALLY: (*Imitating Brer Rabbit's walk.*) Lippity-clippity, clippity-lippity.

JAMES: An' he spied dat Tar-Baby.

SALLY: Mawnin'.

JAMES: Sez Brer Rabbit, sezee.

SALLY: Nice wedder dis mawnin'.

JAMES: Sezee. But de Tar-Baby don't say nuthin'. (*He gives a deaf-and-dumb look, in complete contrast to his animated storytelling.*)

SALLY: What you doin' settin' in the road this fine mawnin'?

JAMES: Sez Brer Rabbit, sezee. But de Tar-Baby ain't sayin' nuthin'. (*Again the look*)

SALLY: Is you deaf? 'Cause if you is, I kin holler louder!

JAMES: Sezee. But de Tar-Baby stay still. (*Again the look*)

SALLY: You're stuck up, dat's what you is. I'm gonna larn you howter talk ter 'spectubble fokes.

JAMES: So Brer Rabbit draw back wid his fis an' "blap!", he—

(SALLY, *in trying to hit* JAMES, *kicks over a pitcher of water.* JEFFERSON *enters and sees her.*)

SALLY: Oh!

JEFFERSON: (*Angrily*) Sally, what are you—?! Are you two playing in here?! My papers—!

JAMES: I'm sorry, Massuh. It's my fault.

JEFFERSON: I told you at the least sign of trouble—

JAMES: I'll clean it right up.

JEFFERSON: No, I need you to start cooking. I am entertaining tonight.

JAMES: But tonight I'm—!

JEFFERSON: Yes, James?

JAMES: Nothin'.

JEFFERSON: Sally can clean up her own mess.

(*He selects a book from the shelf.* JAMES *stands still.*)

JEFFERSON: James, I want to see a menu before I take my walk.

JAMES: (*The obedient slave again*) How many for dinner, Massuh?

JEFFERSON: Fifteen.

(JAMES, *with a last look to* SALLY, *exits.* SALLY *begins mopping up the water.* JEFFERSON *records the daily temperature.*)

JEFFERSON: Sixty-eight . . . Well, Sally, your quarantine is over and you feel perfectly well, just as I promised. Quite a clever idea, really, this vaccination. They make you sick to make you well.

SALLY: (*Suddenly*) I'm sorry James an' me was playin', Master. I didn' mean to make you mad.

JEFFERSON: Nonsense, Sally, I am never angry. To lose control of one's passions is to lose control of one's destiny.

(SALLY *stands trembling and silent.*)

JEFFERSON: Is something wrong?

(*She shakes her head.*)

JEFFERSON: Are you a trifle . . . homesick?

(*She nods.*)

JEFFERSON: Then you must occupy your mind. Remember, the head is stronger than the heart, so you can always overcome despair if you just think hard enough.

SALLY: Think about what?

JEFFERSON: What's something you really love about Monticello?

SALLY: The flowers.

JEFFERSON: Then name me some. That way you can bring a piece of home over here.

SALLY: Well, there's . . . lilies an' . . . buttercups . . . an' daisies an'—what's those purple ones out near the well?

JEFFERSON: Hyacinths.

SALLY: (*Becoming more excited.*) Hyacinths an' violets an' honeysuckle, an' forget-me-nots, an' roses an' gladiators—

JEFFERSON: Gladiolas.

SALLY: An' what was Mistress Martha's favorite? Kept the house full of 'em!

JEFFERSON: Daffodils. Feel better now?

SALLY: Uh-huh. Thank you, Master.

JEFFERSON: (*The problem solved, all business again*) Good. Now, every morning at precisely 6:30 you shall meet me here. The first thing I do every day is soak my feet in ice water to ward off colds. While I soak them, I want you to massage my wrist, which I have severely injured in a fall. Bring over that bowl, fill it up, and we'll begin.

(*During the above* JEFFERSON *has removed his shoes and stockings.* SALLY *places the basin at his feet. As she pours the water, and he begins reading, the lights change to . . .*)

Scene 3

(*The Drawing Room. Winter, 1788. The sound of rain.* SALLY *hums as she massages* JEFFERSON'S *wrist. He is still reading.*)

JEFFERSON: Humming, Sally.

SALLY: Sorry, Master, I forgot.

(*She bathes some more. She hums again.* JEFFERSON *clears his throat. Silence. Then, looking at his book, and mispronouncing it.*)

SALLY: What's King Lear?

JEFFERSON: King *Lear.* It's a play.

(*Beat*)

SALLY: What's it about?

JEFFERSON: Filial duty.

(*Beat*)

SALLY: What did the king do?

JEFFERSON: (*Pointedly*) He had a daughter who questioned him.

(*Beat*)

SALLY: What'd she question him—

JEFFERSON: (*Closing the book.*) My, we are curious this morning! Dry me.

SALLY: Think I could read that book?

JEFFERSON: I doubt it. It's poetry.

(SALLY *dries his feet, then puts on his stockings and shoes. She hums.*)

JEFFERSON: You're always humming, Sally.

SALLY: Mama says it's because a mockin' bird sang on my windowsill the day I was born.

JEFFERSON: That's just a superstition.

SALLY: Ain't you superstitious, Master?

JEFFERSON: It is my considered opinion that superstition is the religion of the feeble-minded. Or perhaps it's Catholicism. Sally, what time did Patsy say she'd return from the convent?

SALLY: She didn'.

JEFFERSON: I don't want her to miss our walk again. That would be the third time this week.

SALLY: She really likes them nuns. Says they are brides of Christ. How'd they get married to Him, Master?

JEFFERSON: Magic. (*He looks at the outside thermometer.*) Thirty degrees.

SALLY: *Il fait froid.*

JEFFERSON: Learning some French, are you, Sally?

SALLY: Not nearly enough. I wish I could get me tutored like James.

JEFFERSON: Oh?

SALLY: Yes, Master. Then when I have to go buy vegetables for James, like today, I'd know what to say, an' soon I could understand them, too, 'cause

you cain't hardly understand 'em, Master, they jab-
ber like a white girl—Oh, I didn' mean—

JEFFERSON: That's all right, Sally.

SALLY: See, what's the good of bein' in a whole
'nuther country if you cain't even talk to people?
Plus which I'd be more use to you an' Miss Patsy an'
everybody. An' when I get home, I can talk French to
all the other slaves!

JEFFERSON: Well, I don't see why you can't be tutored
along with James. It would make you more useful.
Where is he anyway?

SALLY: He ducks out an' comes back all fired up,
shoutin' 'bout "Death to all tyrants!" What's a tyrant?

JEFFERSON: Nothing you should worry about. (*He
looks out the window.*) Rain. How I loathe Paris
winters. (*Crosses to his desk to work.*)

SALLY: Mama says it's good luck when it rains on your
birthday.

JEFFERSON: More superstition, Sally? Besides, it's not
my birthday.

SALLY: No, Master, it's mine.

JEFFERSON: Oh. (*Beat*) Well, happy birthday, Sally.

SALLY: Thank you, Master. The mistress always gave
us a present back home.

JEFFERSON: There is no mistress here.

SALLY: Oh.

(SALLY, *disappointed, crosses to the window and looks
out.*)

JEFFERSON: (*Sensing her disappointment.*) What would
you like for your birthday, Sally?

SALLY: To take a walk in the Bois de Boulogne. I
sneaked off to the woods every chance I got at home,

but here the only place I get to go is the market on days when James is too busy. I'd like to see me a animal again an' sit up 'gainst a tree an' listen to the leaves an' just—be in the woods! I know it's a silly wish, Master, but you asked me.

JEFFERSON: Not so silly. I am a man of the earth, too, Sally, despite all this finery.

SALLY: I know you are, Master. I've seen you in the woods lots of times. I'd hide an' watch you mark a tree or study some ferns or pick some flowers. I sure would like to pick me some!

JEFFERSON: Hmmm. When do you go for your vegetables, Sally?

SALLY: I waits till you leave, in case you need me.

JEFFERSON: Well, since Patsy seems to have abandoned me, we'll go out together and on the way to the market we'll pass through the Bois de Boulogne. If it stops raining.

SALLY: I'll make it stop! Thank you, Master. (*Beat*) What's your favorite flower, Master?

JEFFERSON: (*Returning to his papers.*) I never really thought about it.

SALLY: Forget-me-not's mine. Master, why are they called forget—

JEFFERSON: I really don't have time for your questions, Sally. I shall send for you when I am ready to leave. Now run along.

SALLY: Yes, Master. (*She starts to exit, then turns and speaks.*) Do you think I'm feeble-minded, Master?

JEFFERSON: No, Sally, you seem to be fairly intelligent.

SALLY: That's good, 'cause I was just wonderin' if it's a superstition to plunge your feet into icy water every mornin' to ward off colds!

(SALLY *turns on her heel and exits.* JEFFERSON, *surprised, looks after her and laughs, as the lights change to . . .)*

Scene 4

(PATSY'S *Room. Spring, 1788. Afternoon.* PATSY, *dressed in riding clothes, is imagining music. She dances prettily about the room, spinning, and then curtseying. There is a pile of dresses on a chair, with a corset hidden underneath.)*

PATSY: Oh, no, Monsieur, you flatter me . . . This ring? My father gave it to me. . . . Yes, he loves me very much. . . . Another? Well, perhaps after I have some punch. . . .

(SALLY *enters, carrying a beautiful dress.)*

SALLY: Here you go, Missy. I done tucked an' stretched where we 'greed.

PATSY: Thank you, Sally.

SALLY: Wanna try it on?

PATSY: I can't. Papa's waiting for me to go riding. Isn't this the most beautiful dress?!

SALLY: You sure gon' look a picture, Missy.

PATSY: A real French ball!

SALLY: An' with such a handsome man.

PATSY: I'm sure Monsieur de Lafayette is just paying Papa a promise. But he is very gallant, isn't he?

SALLY: *Oui,* Missy, *très gallant.*

PATSY: I've been practising. Come, I must teach you how so you can be Lafayette. I want to be perfect.

SALLY: All right, but I don't know if us black folks can move that slow.

PATSY: It's easy, just three movements at first. One, two, three . . . (*She demonstrates.*) Try it.

(SALLY *begins to dance.*)

PATSY: That's it, see how easy it is.

(*They dance together.*)

PATSY: But you must carry your head high and back like this. It helps to think of something. I think of horse manure.

(SALLY's *head snaps back.*)

PATSY: Good, Sally. Now you be Lafayette and ask me to dance.

(SALLY *assumes a masculine pose and approaches.*)

SALLY: *Ma charmante mademoiselle, il me donnerait le plus grand plaisir de dancer avec vous.*

PATSY: *Enchanté, Monsieur, enchanté.*

(SALLY *bows grandly,* PATSY *curtsies and they dance. After a moment* PATSY *catches sight of herself in the mirror and stops.*)

PATSY: Oh, look at me, flat as a pancake. When will they grow?!

SALLY: I don't know, Missy, you've got a couple of little mountains startin'.

PATSY: Yes, my "Monticellos!" Promise you won't tell, Sally—if the Sisters knew, they'd die—but I must show you what I've bought. (*She brings out the corset.*)

SALLY: What is it?

PATSY: The latest fashion. See how it lifts? And guess what the French call it? A *divorce!* Now I can have the Alps! Do you think it's too daring?

SALLY: Mama says what the rooster ain't knowin' won't stop his crowin'! Put it on.

PATSY: I don't have time. You put it on, I want to see how it works.

SALLY: Me, Missy?

PATSY: Hurry up. Papa doesn't like it when I'm late.

SALLY: Well, all right.

(SALLY *strips off her blouse. The mistress helps the slave into her piece of French finery.*)

PATSY: Let me just tie it. ... There. ... Now push your breasts up. ... All right, turn around and let's see.

(SALLY *turns and* PATSY *is stunned:* SALLY *looks quite ravishing.*)

PATSY: Sally! (*Beat*) Maybe I ought not wear that. Take it off quick and put it back. I'd better hurry.

(PATSY, *hiding her embarrassment and envy, exits.* SALLY *regards herself in the mirror. She likes what she sees.*)

SALLY: I got the Alps! (*She curtsies prettily, leaning down, exposing her breasts.*) Well, if she don't want it, maybe she'll give it to me.

(SALLY *spins happily about the room. As she does so, the corset drops to her side just as* JEFFERSON *enters, speaking.*)

JEFFERSON: Patsy, why must you keep me waiting like this?!

(*Seeing* SALLY, *he stops. In her surprise she has turned to face him. For one still moment, they look at each other. Then* SALLY *quickly hides her nakedness.* JEFFERSON, *aroused, continues to look hard at her throughout.*)

JEFFERSON: Where is your mistress?

SALLY: She left for the stables.

JEFFERSON: I didn't see her.

SALLY: She went down the back stairs.

JEFFERSON: What is that in your hands?

SALLY: Miss Patsy's new corset.

JEFFERSON: What does she want with a—? Let me see— (*Quickly*) Never mind. (*Beat*) You'd better put some clothes on, Sally, you'll catch cold.

(JEFFERSON *exits.* SALLY *stands still, trembling slightly, as the lights change to . . .*)

Scene 5

(*The Bois de Boulogne. A summer afternoon, 1788.* JEFFERSON *looks at the sky through a small telescope.*)

JEFFERSON: (*Excitedly*) Isn't it unbelievable?! First they rose above the trees, cleared that small mountain, and now they're as high as the clouds and out of sight. In a balloon! Man flew! I tell you, Sally, anything is possible: One day there might be several balloons towing a large platform filled with as many as fifty people! Change, the savior of mankind!

(*He winces from a pain in his neck.* SALLY *enters, carrying her market basket.*)

SALLY: Did you hurt yourself?

JEFFERSON: Just stiff from all that craning.

SALLY: I'll massage it.

JEFFERSON: Perhaps that would help.

SALLY: Sit over here. (*Beat*) You'll have to take off your coat.

JEFFERSON: Oh, yes . . .

(*He does so.* SALLY *pulls out a small bottle from her pocket.*)

JEFFERSON: What's that?

SALLY: One of Mama's healin' potions. She uses it for all kinds of hurts an' pains.

JEFFERSON: Smells dusky.

SALLY: I'm sorry, Master, that's me. I bathe with a soap made from woodash and palm oil.

JEFFERSON: I rather like it. Smells like smoldering fires.

SALLY: Mama says her mama bathed with that soap every day in Africa. Wouldn' you like to do that, Master, bathe every single day?

JEFFERSON: Sounds excessive.

SALLY: Not in the summertime, like now. It's the best way to cool off.

JEFFERSON: So what is in this concoction of your Mama's?

SALLY: I don't know exactly. Lots of things. Ginseng an'—

JEFFERSON: Ginseng? Did you know the Chinese boil ginseng in their tea as an aphrodisiac?

SALLY: What's an aphrodisiac?

JEFFERSON: Something that stimulates the senses.

SALLY: You mean it makes you see or hear better?

JEFFERSON: (*A bit uncomfortable with the topic*) No, it makes one more ardent—supposedly.

SALLY: What's ardent?

JEFFERSON: Well . . . well, I suppose the French would say "amoureux."

SALLY: Oh! (*Excited, she massages him vigorously.*)

JEFFERSON: Not so hard.

SALLY: Sorry, Master, but sometimes you've got to make it hurt to make it heal. Sort of like a vaccination.

JEFFERSON: Is that why James calls you Rabbit, because you're so clever?

SALLY: Mama says us black folks is clever 'cause we ain't got so many books piled on our heads our brains cain't move.

JEFFERSON: Your Mama has a great many sayings, doesn't she?

SALLY: *Beaucoup.*

JEFFERSON: *Et comment va le français? Tu apprends bien?*

SALLY: *Oui. Et le professeur dit que j'ai un vrai accent Parisien.*

JEFFERSON: You've learned a great deal in a year. I wish I had your accent.

SALLY: I could teach you.

JEFFERSON: Teach me?

SALLY: How to speak French *comme un vrai Parisien.*

JEFFERSON: That *would* be a miracle.

SALLY: Don't you believe in miracles?

JEFFERSON: No.

SALLY: Today man flew.

(*Beat*)

JEFFERSON: You're right, Sally. If man can fly, then Thomas Jefferson can speak French *comme un vrai Parisien.*

SALLY: The first lesson is how to say the French "U" as in "Tu."

JEFFERSON: Tu.

SALLY: Not "OO," "U." *Tu.*

JEFFERSON: (*Mispronouncing it.*) *Tu.*

SALLY: Whistle.

(JEFFERSON *whistles.*)

SALLY: Now, keeping your lips in a whistle, say "EE."

(JEFFERSON *tries the sound.* SALLY *touches his lips and forms them properly. He tries the sound again.*)

SALLY: Better. *Tu, tu, tu.*

JEFFERSON: *Tu, tu, tu.*

SALLY: Good. *Tu.*

JEFFERSON: *Tu.*

SALLY: *Tu!*

JEFFERSON: *Tu!*

(*They both begin saying the word in machinegun-like bursts until they collapse into laughter.*)

SALLY: You see, Master. Anything is possible, like you said.

JEFFERSON: I'm more convinced now than ever.

SALLY: We'll have another lesson tomorrow.

JEFFERSON: I shall like that. (*He gazes at her fondly.*) Well . . . (*Beat. Then he rises with his coat.*) Well, I should get to work. I want to record my thoughts on today's miracle. Both of them. And you have your vegetables to buy.

SALLY: (*Helping him with the coat.*) Yes, Master.

JEFFERSON: Run along then.

(SALLY *starts to exit. He calls anxiously.*)

JEFFERSON: I shall see you in the morning, as usual.

SALLY: Yes, Master, as usual.

(SALLY *exits.* JEFFERSON *looks after her. Slowly he touches his lips as* SALLY *had done and says softly:*)

JEFFERSON: *Tu.*

(*Lively music is heard as the lights change to* . . .)

Scene 6

(*A Diplomatic Ball. August, 1788. Evening. The Ballroom and Drawing Room.* PATSY *and* LAFAYETTE *enter in mid-dance from opposite sides of the stage and dance to Center. There they bow and curtsy, not to each other but to their respective "partners".* JAMES *passes, offering drinks to the "guests". There should be the sound and feeling of a large crowd, though only the principal characters are visible.*)

LAFAYETTE: Ah, Jimmy! (*To* PATSY) *Champagne?*

PATSY: (*Looking around.*) Well, since Papa's not around.

(*They both take drinks from* JAMES' *tray.*)

LAFAYETTE: And how is *mon ami, le chef,* this evening?

JAMES: Fine, Master Lafa—

LAFAYETTE: Ah, ah, remember our pact.

JAMES: *Monsieur* Lafayette.

LAFAYETTE: You look very handsome.

JAMES: I didn' want to get all gussied up, but Massuh made me.

LAFAYETTE: Yes . . . My compliments on your *hors d'oeuvres. Superbe!* You must leave this tyrant and come work for me.

JAMES: I'd like that, Monsieur, but I ain't free to leave. 'Scuse me.

(JAMES *moves off, serving "guests".* LAFAYETTE *looks after him, disturbed.*)

LAFAYETTE: (*Quietly*) Perhaps one day soon, Jimmy.

(JEFFERSON *appears, passing among his "guests", nodding and engaging in silent conversations.*)

PATSY: You sure are nice to James.

LAFAYETTE: I like him. Sally, too. (*Toasting*) À votre beauté!

(*They clink glasses and drink, then move away as the music signals another dance.*)

LAFAYETTE: And how was your dance with Baron Montard?

PATSY: I fear the Baron dances better with his words than his feet.

LAFAYETTE: A common affliction among many diplomats, Mademoiselle, your father included, perhaps.

PATSY: Since Mama died, my father doesn't dance at all.

LAFAYETTE: A pity. Ah, there is our illustrious host now. *Pardonnez-moi,* but I must speak with your father.

PATSY: But, Monsieur, you have yet to dance with me.

LAFAYETTE: I was merely saving the best for last, Mademoiselle.

PATSY: If you think you can win me over with your famous French flattery—I'll give you five minutes.

(LAFAYETTE *kisses her hand and they part. He approaches* JEFFERSON. *At some point,* SALLY *begins to wander about the party serving hors d'oeuvres.*)

LAFAYETTE: Enjoying your party?

JEFFERSON: (*Smiling and nodding to "guests" as he talks.*) No, I have concluded that there are three species of creatures who seem coming when they are going, going when they come: diplomats, women, and crabs.

LAFAYETTE: Then you should feel right at home.

(JEFFERSON *gives him a questioning look.*)

LAFAYETTE: Snuff?

JEFFERSON: You never give up, do you?

LAFAYETTE: No.

JEFFERSON: I have just checked my thermometer: seventy-five degrees, at night! This August shall be worse than last. And far too hot for the Finance Minister. I hear he has resigned.

LAFAYETTE: People are starving. Even the rich are affected. Yesterday I received an invitation to an elegant dinner with a note attached: "And please bring your own bread." Soon there will be riots.

JEFFERSON: Such turmoil undermines all my negotiations. Is there no middle ground where reason can hold sway?

LAFAYETTE: No. In France every man is either the hammer or the anvil.

JEFFERSON: What will happen?

LAFAYETTE: As you have said, *mon ami*, the tree of liberty must be refreshed from time to time with the blood of patriots and tyrants. It is its natural manure.

JEFFERSON: You must not allow that! All that is needed is a standard to which all three estates can adhere. Your charter for the rights of man.

LAFAYETTE: I cannot finish it.

JEFFERSON: You must. I will do everything to help you, privately. Have I not already sent you pages of notes on—

LAFAYETTE: Then finish it yourself. It takes a better hypocrit than I.

JEFFERSON: What do you mean?

(SALLY *approaches*.)

SALLY: Excuse me, *Maitre*, but Madame Roulet wishes to introduce you to the Italian diplomat.

JEFFERSON: Wonderful. Another crab. (*To* LAFAYETTE.) Meet me shortly in my drawing room where we can discuss this more privately and, I trust, more fruitfully. (*He exits*.)

LAFAYETTE: *Tu es charmante, ce soir, Sally. C'est une nouvelle robe?*

SALLY: Master bought it so I could look like a proper French maid.

LAFAYETTE: How kind of him.

(PATSY *begins dancing with another "guest".*)

SALLY: Miss Patsy been dancin' up a storm. She's havin' a fine time!

LAFAYETTE: Are you?

SALLY: *Oui, Monsieur*. This is my first diplomatic ball! *Hors d'oeuvres?*

LAFAYETTE: *Non, merci.*

(LAFAYETTE *goes to the Drawing Room, where he takes out his snuff box and takes some snuff, leaving the box on the desk.* JAMES *spots* SALLY *and they teasingly offer each other their wares.*)

JAMES: *Champagne?!*

SALLY: *Hors d'oeuvres?!*

JEFFERSON: (*Calling as she passes.*) Sally!

SALLY: Yes, Master?

JEFFERSON: Bring a bottle of my best red to the drawing room.

(*As she starts off.*)

JEFFERSON: Ah . . . is that your new dress?

SALLY: *Oui.*

JEFFERSON: *Charmante.*

SALLY: *Merci.*

JEFFERSON: If your mama could see you now, eh? Monticello seems very far away, doesn't it?

SALLY: Yes, it does.

JEFFERSON: Enjoying yourself?

SALLY: Oh, yes, Master. Are you?

JEFFERSON: Yes, I am.

SALLY: Then how come you ain't dancin'?

JEFFERSON: I don't dance.

SALLY: You used to.

JEFFERSON: Yes, I did.

SALLY: You know somethin' Mama told me once, Master? James an' me had caught a rabbit—James shined a lantern in his eyes an' he froze, just trapped in that light—, an' we brought him home an' I tamed that rabbit, had him so's he'd eat right out of my hand an' sit on my lap—Lord, he was fine! An' then he died, an' I carried on an' carried on for weeks, till finally Mama had to sit me down an' say, "Now lissen here, Sally Hemings, you got to learn one thing in life, 'specially if you's a slave. The earth belongs to the livin'. The dead's got no rights over it. Now you forget that rabbit an' go 'bout your business." But you know, Master, I reckon that's somethin' white folks got to learn as well as colored. (*Beat*) I'll fetch the wine.

(SALLY *moves off.* JEFFERSON *watches her go, transfixed. Then he enters the drawing room.*)

JEFFERSON: Well, sir, you were speaking of hypocrisy?

LAFAYETTE: How can you, whose valor, wisdom, and virtue have done so much in ameliorating the condition of mankind—

JEFFERSON: My friend, if you'll—

LAFAYETTE: Live in the midst of an abomination like slavery and do nothing?!

JEFFERSON: Do nothing?!! Do nothing. . . . My dear Marquis, when I was twenty-six and first elected to the state legislature, I introduced a bill to make it legal for slave owners to free their slaves—for the which I was roundly booed and hissed from the hall. As a lawyer, I attempted to win freedom for a mulatto who was legally "white"—the judge peremptorily dismissed my suit. As chairman of the committee on Virginia's western lands, I proposed that slavery be outlawed from the territories—defeated by a single vote. And in my famous Declaration, you will *not* find the passage accusing George III of waging "cruel war against human beings, capturing and carrying them into slavery in another hemisphere," because it was struck out at the insistence of Georgia and South Carolina and the acquiescence of all else!

LAFAYETTE: And so you deserted the field?

JEFFERSON: I shall never desert the field. But as I was silently listening to the delegates tear my precious words to tatters, Dr. Franklin pulled me aside and said, "Mr. Jefferson, it's hot, and there are too many flies." I was speaking of human bondage, and he, of flies.

LAFAYETTE: *Imbecile!*

JEFFERSON: No, he was right. He knew that if politics is your mistress, compromise is your bed.

LAFAYETTE: This from the author of the Declaration of Independence!!

JEFFERSON: Nature, habit, deep-rooted prejudice, all have drawn indelible lines of distinction between the races, lines your pretty gallantries will never erase. I told you, at the proper time—

(LAFAYETTE *turns away in disgust.* SALLY *enters with wine.*)

SALLY: Your wine, Master.

JEFFERSON: Put it down over there.

(PATSY *hurries in.*)

PATSY: Papa, everyone is asking for you. And you, Monsieur, owe me a dance.

LAFAYETTE: Pretty gallantries, sir?

(*He leads* PATSY *next to* SALLY.)

PATSY: What are you doing?

LAFAYETTE: I am asking your father a simple question. Here you have two women, one white, the other . . . Well, you tell me, sir, just what it is exactly that distinguishes these two. Sally, I would like to have the honor of this dance.

SALLY: Oh, no, Monsieur, I cain't dance with you.

LAFAYETTE: Why not?

SALLY: It's not right.

LAFAYETTE: It is very right, Sally.

SALLY: I don't know how.

LAFAYETTE: Patsy tells me you have been practising her. I am sure you will dance exquisitely.

SALLY: Master?

LAFAYETTE: You needn't look to him, Sally. He will not stop you. Come.

(LAFAYETTE *leads* SALLY *out and they begin to dance a stately minuet. He dances nobly, proudly. She dances with fear and apprehension, but nevertheless delicately, gracefully, and, indeed, exquisitely.* JEFFERSON *watches from his doorway,* PATSY *at his side.* SALLY *can feel his penetrating eyes, but she avoids his look. We sense that the "guests" pull back and watch* SALLY *and* LAFAYETTE *dance alone.* JAMES *enters, is surprised, then watches his sister proudly.*)

PATSY: Papa, dance with me. Please!

JEFFERSON: No, daughter . . .

(PATSY *hurries off.* SALLY *and* LAFAYETTE *dance on. Making a turn, she looks up and meets* JEFFERSON'S *stare.* SALLY *runs from the stage.* LAFAYETTE *straightens, looks at* JEFFERSON, *clicks his heels, and walks proudly away.* JAMES *runs after his sister. The music stops. We sense the "guests" leaving.* JEFFERSON *looks after* SALLY, *then speaks quietly.*)

JEFFERSON: I don't dance . . .

(JEFFERSON *returns to his desk. He finds* LAFAYETTE'S *snuffbox. For a moment he stares at the erotically naked woman painted on the box. Then he opens it, takes some snuff, and snorts it. As* JEFFERSON *sits, pours himself some wine, and drinks it down, the lights change to . . .*)

Scene 7

(SALLY'S *room in the attic. A bell sounds 2* A.M. SALLY, *carrying a candle, enters in her nightgown. Her hair falls beautifully about her shoulders as she sets down the candle and stands by the small window, bathed in moonlight. For a moment she closes her eyes, perhaps in prayer, then opens them and stands still, waiting. After a moment,* JEFFERSON *enters and stands, staring at her. He looks dishevelled from a sleepless night.*)

SALLY: (*Without turning*) I been waitin' for you, Master.

JEFFERSON: Waiting, Sally?

SALLY: The way you looked at me tonight. Mama told me 'bout that look.

(SALLY *turns. She unties her nightgown and it drops to the floor, revealing her nakedness.* JEFFERSON *takes her in his arms, kissing her passionately. As his hands move over her body,* SALLY *gasps.*)

SALLY: Master!

(*As the lights quickly change to . . .*)

Scene 8

(*The Drawing Room. Early the next morning.* JAMES *prepares for the daily bathing, moving* JEFFERSON'S *chair into place and setting the necessary bowls and towels. He is whistling the opening of the* Marseillaise. *Finished, he looks anxiously through the telescope, then turns back into the room, delighted. He waits impatiently for* SALLY *and is about to go search for her when she scurries in with her pitcher.*)

JAMES: Where you been? It's late.

SALLY: Has the master been lookin' for me?

JAMES: He done overslept, too. Maybe now he'll stop tellin' us, "The sun never yet caught me in bed." (*Beat*) Oh, Sally, you looked so beautiful last night. If

Mama could have seen you—*un, deux, trois, un deux, trois!*—she might have jumped up an' danced herself!

SALLY: What you so happy 'bout?

JAMES: Meetin' tonight. An' you comin' with me.

SALLY: Oh, Brother, I don't know nothin' 'bout politics.

JAMES: Then you better learn. What you think's keepin' you in chains? An' there ain't but one way to break them chains. Ask that ol' revolutionary, Thomas Jefferson.

SALLY: He's gonna catch you one day, an'—

JAMES: An' punish us? I told you, Sally, we Hemingses have got Wayles blood in us, the blood of his dear, departed wife.

SALLY: Don't forget it's Wayles blood that's made you a cook instead of a cotton-picker.

JAMES: I wish to God I could forget! But I remember, Rabbit, oh, yeah. I remember how me an' Isaac used to steal chickens. We musta wrung the necks of dozens of them birds 'fore ol' Bacon caught us one night comin' outa the henhouse. "Git on home, Hemings!" he says to me. But he takes poor lil' Isaac off to the whippin' post right then an' there. An' as I was layin' in bed I could hear the whip crackin' 'cross Isaac's back—crack! crack!—'cross that poor darkey's back. That's all I heard, though, 'cause Isaac never let out a sound. It was me who was screamin', screamin' from my bed in the Big House, screamin' inside—knowin' the blood runnin' down that poor field hand's back was just as red as mine.

SALLY: That was the overseer's doin'. The master dudn' believe in whippin'.

JAMES: No, he believes in freedom an' equality!

SALLY: He's a kind man an' you know it!

JAMES: I got a book of Jefferson's I want you to read, Rabbit. Then let's see how kind you think he is.

SALLY: I don't care about your book an' I don't care what you think about him!

JAMES: What's the matter with you?

SALLY: Just leave me alone.

JAMES: I ain't gonna leave you alone till you—

(*As* JEFFERSON *enters,* JAMES *immediately switches gears.*)

JAMES: Oh, mawnin', Massuh. How come you slept so late? Ain't like you. Reckon you musta enjoyed yourself more 'n' you intended last night.

(JEFFERSON *shoots a look at* SALLY, *but she averts her eyes. He begins removing his shoes and stockings.*)

JAMES: You got to watch out for that champagne, Massuh. Some things go down easy, but come back hard. Well, I best be gettin' to the kitchen. (*He starts to exit, stops.*) Oh, you ain't got any surprise visitors for me tonight, has you, Massuh?

JEFFERSON: No.

JAMES: (*With a wicked smile*) Good.

(*He exits.* JEFFERSON *plunges his feet into the bowl of water. He and* SALLY *are silent, avoiding each other's looks.* SALLY *timidly takes his wrist to massage it.*)

JEFFERSON: Not today, Sally.

SALLY: *Oui, Maitre.*

(*After a moment,* JEFFERSON *impatiently pulls his feet from the bowl and begins to towel them dry.* SALLY *quickly bends to help.*)

SALLY: I'll do it, Master. It's my job.

(JEFFERSON *sits tensely as she dries his feet. She rolls his stockings over his knees as he stiffens, tortured by her touch. She sings softly.*)

SALLY:
"Drink to me only with thine eyes,
An' I will pledge with mine.
Or leave a kiss within—"

JEFFERSON: That'll do.

SALLY: Wait, I got to finish. "Never leave a task undone," ain't that what you're always tellin' me?
"Or leave a kiss within the cup
An' I'll not ask for wine."

JEFFERSON: That's enough. (*He bends to help her.*)

SALLY: "The thirst that from the soul doth rise—"

JEFFERSON: (*Moving violently away, whether completely dressed or not.*) I said that's enough! Enough massaging and humming and speaking French and singing my wife's songs.

SALLY: Master, I ain't mean to—

JEFFERSON: And why can't you learn to speak English? If you speak French *comme un vrai Parisien*, why must we have these interminable "ain'ts?!" Ain't, ain't, ain't ain't!!!

SALLY: I'm sorry, Master, I—

JEFFERSON: And stop this constant apologizing! Be responsible for your actions!

SALLY: Yes, Master.

(*Beat.* JEFFERSON *finishes dressing.*)

JEFFERSON: I am going away. It is time I saw more of *la belle France* than its sinful cities.

SALLY: I shall miss you. (*She gathers up her things.*) Master, you won't have nobody to bathe you on your trip, will you?

JEFFERSON: I suppose not.

SALLY: Good.

(JEFFERSON *goes to the doorway, then turns.*)

JEFFERSON: God, Sally, it's frightening how much you resemble her sometimes.

SALLY: We did have the same father, Master.

(JEFFERSON *exits.* SALLY *pulls a letter from her apron and moves downstage as the lights change to . . .*)

Scene 9

(PATSY'S *Room* (*or The Drawing Room*). *Several weeks later. Morning.* SALLY *is reading a letter.*)

SALLY:" . . . In my last letter, I mentioned that I find the arts in general worth seeing but not studying. I have, however, just discovered two exquisite exceptions. The first is Van Der Werf's painting of Sarah delivering Hagar up to Abraham. The look on Hagar's face—a terrifying combination of fear and defiance—touched something deep within me, a chord of both pity and shame. Equally haunting is the Maison Quarée at Nimes . . ."

(PATSY *calls from offstage, then runs on, carrying her books, a brush, and a mirror.*)

PATSY: (*Offstage*) Sally! A letter from Papa at last!

(SALLY *quickly stuffs her letter in her apronstrings.*)

SALLY: Good, Missy. Read it to me.

PATSY: All right. But you must hurry with my hair. I can't be late today, there's a Latin test.

(*Reads as* SALLY *combs her hair.*)

PATSY: "Dear Patsy, I have not received a letter from you in some time. This is far short of my injunction to write once a week. I wish to know how you come on in your writing. Take care that you never spell a word wrong. It produces great praise in a lady to spell well—" (*Interjects*) Oh, Papa! (*Continues*) "I omitted in my last letter to advise you on the subject of dress. Above all things, let your clothes be clean, whole, and properly put on. Nothing is so disgusting to our sex as a want of cleanliness and delicacy in yours—" (*Interjects*) Oh, really, Papa! (*Continues*) "Remember that a mind always employed is always happy. Remember, too, that the more you learn, the more I love you. Adieu, my dear child. Lose no moment in improving your head, nor any opportunity of exercising your heart in benevolence. Yours affectionately, Thomas Jefferson."

SALLY: Nothin' 'bout comin' home? He's been gone awful long.

PATSY: No. He might at least have told me what he was doing.

SALLY: Missy, who was Hagar?

PATSY: Sarah's slave. Sarah couldn't have children, so she gave Hagar to Abraham to conceive with. Can you imagine doing that, Sally?

SALLY: Depends on Abraham!

(PATSY *picks up a Latin book and reads.*)

PATSY: *Non omnis moriar. Multaque pars mei, vitavit Libitinam.* "I shall not wholly die, what's best of me shall 'scape the tomb." If you ask me, what's worst of him 'scaped.

SALLY: Who said that?

PATSY: Horace.

SALLY: There's a slave named Horace at Monticello. He speaks Latin, too.

PATSY: How would Horace know any Latin?

SALLY: I don't know, but he does. He spouts it when he's conjurin'.

PATSY: Sally, you don't believe in that voo-doo, do you?

SALLY: Don't you believe in all those saints you're always prayin' to?

PATSY: That's different, they're real. They were blessed by God with a vision.

SALLY: Horace had a vision. An angel came to him, yanked a wildworm root straight out of the ground, laid it 'crost his hands, an' said, "Go, Horace, an' heal thy people with this root!"

PATSY: Oh, Sally, if only you poor Negroes were educated.

SALLY: Well, what's the difference 'tween the root 'roun' Horace's neck an' that medallion you got 'roun' yours?

PATSY: The difference is, one is a holy medal blessed by the Pope, representing hundreds of years of Christianity, and the other is a pagan charm, conjured over by a trickster, representing the superstitions of your ancestors in Africa.

SALLY: Well, I think—

PATSY: I really don't have time, Sally. You couldn't possibly understand if I explained it forever. Fetch my bonnet.

SALLY: Yes'm.

(PATSY *spies* SALLY's *letter.*)

PATSY: What's that sticking out of your apron, Sally?

SALLY: Nothin'. You better hurry, Miss Patsy.

PATSY: Let me see it.

SALLY: You'll be late.

PATSY: Let me see it.

SALLY: What for?

PATSY: Because I want to.

SALLY: But it's mine, Miss Patsy.

PATSY: *Yours*, Sally?

(PATSY *holds out her hand.* SALLY *gives her the letter.*)

PATSY: This is Papa's hand!

SALLY: (*Quickly*) Yes'm, Miss Patsy. He writes me sometimes in French, so I can practice it, so I can be a proper maid for a fine young lady like yourself. See, it's in French.

PATSY: Yes, I see.

SALLY: It's just a silly little letter.

PATSY: I doubt very much if Papa is capable of writing a "silly little letter." How many has he written you?

SALLY: I don't know, Missy. Not many.

PATSY: And just whom are you going to speak French with back at Monticello, Sally? Horace? (*She tears the letter in two.*) When I return from school, I want you waiting in my room. I've work for you to do.

(PATSY *exits.* SALLY *picks up the pieces of the letter and reads.*)

SALLY: ". . . the Maison Quarée at Nimes. I am but a son of nature, loving what I see an' feel, without being able to give reason, nor carin' much whether there be one. Here I am, gazin' whole hours at this exquisite building, like a lover at his mistress . . ." (*Beat*) Like a lover at his mistress.

(SALLY *holds the letter to her breast. Offstage we hear* JAMES *singing as the lights change to* ...)

Scene 10

(*The Drawing Room. July 14, 1789. Dusk.* JAMES *enters, singing. He is bloodied and dishevelled, carrying a pike, and is wearing the red, white, and blue cockade of the Revolution.*)

JAMES: "*Aux armes, mes citoyens! Formez vos bataillions. Marchons! Marchons! Qu'un sang impure abreuve nos sillons!*"

(*As he enters,* SALLY *speaks to him.*)

SALLY: James, where have you been all day?! Are you drunk?

JAMES: On the blood of my oppressors! Rabbit, we attacked the Bastille!

SALLY: Who?

JAMES: Thousands of us—with pitchforks, broomsticks, anything we could find! We stood there cursing those great stone walls, cannon boomin' back at us, hour after hour. An' then we were in! Flingin' open the cells, huggin' an' dancin'—an' someone stuck up a pike with the prison governor's head on it! (*He shouts, remembering the moment, and pulls out a knife.*) Bâtard! Bâtard! (*He sinks his knife into a wall.*) The noise, Rabbit! It lifted you off the ground, surroundin' you like an echo that won't stop. We followed that pike through the streets like it was Jesus leadin' us to the promised land. An' in the houses you could see the bluebloods' faces frozen against their finery: pale, like death, an' white. So white! From naked, shiverin' fear! Of us—us! An' I couldn't help grinnin', thinkin' how for the first time I actually enjoyed seein' the color white!

SALLY: Sit down. I'll get somethin' to eat.

JAMES: There's no time for that. Where's Jefferson?

SALLY: Dining at Madame de Corny—! James, is it safe for the master out—

JAMES: What do you care? This is the servants' day! *Liberté! Fraternité! Egalité!*

SALLY: You actin' crazy!

JAMES: You gonna be actin' crazy, too, soon's you hear my news. You ready to dance, Rabbit? You ready to jump an' shout an' have your heart bust wide open?

SALLY: What is it?

JAMES: Listen good, Rabbit, you ain't never gonna hear a sweeter sound: Sally Hemings, you an' me is legally free.

SALLY: Free?

JAMES: You an' me is standin' on the free soil of France, where slavery is against the law!

SALLY: What?! Who told you this?

JAMES: Not your kind, kind master, that's for sure. None other than the Marquis de Lafayette, God bless his guilty soul. *Vive la France!*

SALLY: An' there ain't nothin' we got to do?

JAMES: Just claim it.

SALLY: (*Trying the word.*) Free . . . Free . . . Oh, James!

(*He lifts her and whirls her around*)

SALLY: FREEEEEEEEEEEEEE!!!!!!!!!!!!! James, if it's true, really true, then Jesus has done reached out of the sky, scooped us up, an' dropped us in that field of flowers at last. Smell the air! Fill your nostrils with it, Brother. Ain't a sweeter smell in all the world!

JAMES: I cain't wait to tell the master.

SALLY: The master? . . .

JAMES: I'm gonna march right up to him an' say, "Jefferson, I wanna talk—"

SALLY: No!

JAMES: What do you mean, "no"?

SALLY: You mean tell him tonight?

JAMES: Soon's he gets home. We're sayin' *au revoir* to Massuh Tom.

SALLY: We cain't leave tonight, James. We . . . we're not ready.

JAMES: We been ready from the first breath, it's him that ain't been ready!

SALLY: But where will we go, how will we eat?

JAMES: Lafayette's done offered me a job. Rabbit, you almost sound like you wanna stay.

SALLY: No, I wanna be free! Just the word on my lips feels like honey an' fire. But . . . this isn't the right time!

JAMES: It's the day we been waitin' for our whole lives! The world's turnin' upside down an' all you care about's clingin' to your master's britches?! What's gotten into you, Sally?

SALLY: Nothin'.

JAMES: Don't lie to me, Sister.

(*A long pause*)

SALLY: All right, James. But you got to promise to listen real good, real good an' hard an' not go yellin' all around, all right?

(JAMES *nods.*)

SALLY: An' you've got to understand, James. Please, please, please, try to understand. (*Beat*) I am with child.

JAMES: What?!

SALLY: Now just calm down an' listen to me—

JAMES: Who did it to you? One of the servants?

SALLY: Nobody "did it to me." I wanted it—

JAMES: What's his name?

SALLY: James—

JAMES: Is he gonna marry you?

SALLY: Please just listen!

JAMES: I'll listen as soon as you tell me his name.

SALLY: I will, but first let me ex—

JAMES: WHAT IS HIS NAME??!!

(*A long pause*)

SALLY: It's the master. (*Quickly*) Now, James, I know what you're thinkin', but it's not true. I wanted it to happen. He was gentle an' lovin' an'—

(JAMES *hits* SALLY *hard on the face, knocking her down.*)

JAMES: You whore! You little black pickaninny whore! So you spread your thighs for the master, did you? You let that pig rut 'roun' in you till he'd had his fill an' went back to his silk sheets an' soft pillows an' left you with another nigger slave in your belly, is that it?!

SALLY: It wasn't like that!

JAMES: Shut up! You tell your little child what it was like, how soft his kisses, how gentle his hands. Tell him that when he's pickin' cotton twelve hours a day, or when you serve him a fine meal of fatback every night. Tell him that when he's sick an' shiverin' but there's not enough covers to go 'roun'. Best of all, tell him that when he's standin' on the auction block cryin', "Please don't let 'em sell me, Mama!" You tell him, Sally Hemings, an' wait for him to say, "Thank you, Mama, for birthin' me." You gonna wait a long time.

SALLY: He will thank me, James. 'Cause he's gonna grow up in the Big House, read the master's books, learn a trade, an' be able to make it in the white man's world.

JAMES: You could stay here an' he'd be born free!

SALLY: I'm stayin' with the master. When he's holdin' me, kissin' an' strokin' me, that's the only place I wanna be.

JAMES: Dreams, Rabbit!

SALLY: He loves me, James.

JAMES: (*With total loathing*) How can you stand to even touch him?

SALLY: Because I love him.

(JAMES *runs off*, SALLY *calling after*.)

SALLY: An' he loves me. He loves me, James! You'll see he loves me! He loves me! He loves me! He loves me!

(SALLY *rocks herself as she cries softly, soothing herself with "He loves me. . . ." After a moment,* JEF- FERSON *calls from offstage:*)

JEFFERSON: Sally?! Sally, where are you?! (*He enters.*) They are rioting in town. It may be dangerous—(*Seeing her on the floor.*) Sally, what is it?

SALLY: I'm scared.

JEFFERSON: (*Taking her in his arms.*) Oh, Sally, Sally. . . . There is nothing to fear. We shall return to Monticello as I said, sit by the fire, walk in the woods, and be safe from all the sorrows of the world.

SALLY: And our child?

JEFFERSON: Will be strong and wise and beautiful, just like his mother. I shall take care of you, Sally. I promise.

SALLY: Oh, Master!

JEFFERSON: (*Gently*) Didn't we agree you are not to call me that in private?

SALLY: Yes . . ., Thomas.

(SALLY *manages a small smile.* JEFFERSON *cradles her in his arms while the gunfire and cannon crescendo around them.*)

End of Act One

ACT TWO

Scene 1

(*The Front Porch and Yard, Monticello. Late afternoon, near sunset, May, 1796.* JEFFERSON's *architectural drawings are on a table. In the dark we hear singing.*)

SALLY:
Meet me, Jesus, meet me
Meet me in the middle of the air
So's if my wings should fail me,
Meet me with another pair.

(*The lights come up to reveal* SALLY *shucking corn on the porch. She is very pregnant, near term. She is dressed in very good clothing for a slave, and wears a set of keys around her waist.*)

SALLY: . . . Better make it two pair, big as I am! Lord, chile, I sure will be glad when you and me parts company. An' your grandmama used to tell me babies came out of holler logs. Spent half my childhood lookin' up dead tree trunks! (*She finds a red ear of corn.*) Well, well, lookee here.

(*She tucks it into her apron.* JEFFERSON *enters, very dirty.*)

JEFFERSON: Finished!

SALLY: Thomas Jefferson, you look like *you* been planted!

JEFFERSON: I couldn't stop myself. I planted carnation, marigold, globe amaranth, auricula, Dutch violet, cockscomb, hathyrus, lilac, Spanish broom, laurel—and I found a field of your favorites. (*He hands her some flowers.*)

SALLY: Forget-me-nots! Thank you, Thomas.

(*He goes to a thermometer hanging on a column and records the temperature in a small notebook.*)

JEFFERSON: Ninety degrees. If this keeps up it will be the hottest summer in seven years. Be sure to stay out of the sun.

SALLY: *You* the redhead!

(*He scratches his head vigorously.*)

SALLY: Sit down and lemme have another go at those lice.

(*JEFFERSON sits at SALLY's feet and she attacks the lice in his hair.*)

SALLY: What brought on this passion for plantin' anyway?

JEFFERSON: Those excellent articles by James Callendar in yesterday's newspaper, denouncing Adams and Hamilton for the monarchists they are. I don't know who is worse: Adams, who equates political dissent with anarchy and lawlessness, or Hamilton, who thinks Julius Caesar the greatest man who ever lived!

SALLY: An' you're just gonna sit here on your mountain an' let them destroy your precious republic?

JEFFERSON: You know how it was when I was Secretary of State. Washington preferred Hamilton to me. And I prefer my beloved Monticello to the lies and calumny that are a politician's constant companions. I'm too old, my ideas too out-of-fashion—

(*SALLY deliberately pulls out a louse, harder than necessary.*)

JEFFERSON: Ow!

SALLY: Sorry, Thomas. But when you go to rootin' out the bad its gonna cost you some pain. (*Holding up the louse.*) Now, here's John Adams. I want you to step on him. (*Puts the louse at JEFFERSON's feet.*) Go on!

(JEFFERSON *squashes the louse delightedly.*)

SALLY: So much for His Rotundancy! How do you feel?

JEFFERSON: Fulfilled!

SALLY: Thomas, this country needs you. Your ideas will never be out of fashion. Trouble is, enough of 'em ain't *in* fashion! (*Corrects herself, smiling*) *Aren't* in fashion.

JEFFERSON: What would you have me do?

SALLY: Let Madison submit your name for the presidency.

JEFFERSON: Well, I never said he couldn't, I just never said he could, and Jemmy's too smart a politician to ask me directly. Silence has its virtues, Sally.

SALLY: Especially when you can get men like Callendar to fight your battles for you.

JEFFERSON: You'd make a good politician, Sally Hemings. Well, the first step will be to encourage Mr. Callendar to keep his pen pointed at the Federalists. I shall send him fifty dollars as a reward.

SALLY: Now, Thomas, there is no need for you to be sending money to strangers when you don't even have enough to finish your own house.

JEFFERSON: I shall borrow it.

SALLY: You already owe—

JEFFERSON: I am determined to build the best house in America, Sally. It shall be like the body of a beautiful woman: light, elegant, exquisitely proportioned, containing hidden mysteries. I want to show my countrymen that a house can be more than mere shelter from the elements. It can be a work or art, a living monument to one's ideals and aspirations.

SALLY: Am I your model, exquisitely proportioned? (*She juts out her stomach.*)

JEFFERSON: You are! (*He goes to study his drawings.*)

SALLY: You know, Thomas, you might get this place built a lot faster if you had some more help. Tom is already seven years old. Don't you think it's time he learned a trade?

JEFFERSON: Perhaps.

SALLY: I thought you might show him how to work the forge, makin' nails. Maybe he could be a kind of apprentice architect to you. You know how he likes to draw.

JEFFERSON: (*Lost in his work*) Hmmm . . .

SALLY: You promised you'd teach our children a trade, remember?

JEFFERSON: Yes, Sally, I remember. He does draw well. Maybe he could be a fine draughtsman some day.

SALLY: (*Persisting*) Or an architect.

JEFFERSON: Or an architect. Where is he?

SALLY: Waitin' at the naillery door.

JEFFERSON: I should have known!

SALLY: Well, I got to start bakin'.

JEFFERSON: That's right, Isaac's getting married tomorrow.

SALLY: An' I'm supplyin' the cake an' broom.

JEFFERSON: What's the broom for again?

SALLY: The preacher-man says a blessin', an' you promise to love each other "till death or distance do you part." Then you stand behind the broom, hold hands, an' jump over it. An' to get un-married all you do is jump back!

JEFFERSON: Would you like to jump over the broom some day, Sally?

SALLY: Yes, Thomas, I would.

JEFFERSON: (*Taking her in his arms.*) This is the moment, when all is peace and harmony, that I should miss most. (*Feels the ear of corn in her apron.*) What's this?

SALLY: A little surprise I found us.

JEFFERSON: (*Removing it.*) Ah, another red ear. And the custom is you get to kiss whomever you choose?

SALLY: Uh-huh.

JEFFERSON: Well, it looks as if in this election I am the only candidate.

SALLY: Uh-huh.

(*They kiss, then* JEFFERSON *holds her in his arms.*)

JEFFERSON: You sure you don't just keep finding the same one?

SALLY: (*Meaning "no"*) Huh-hunh!

(JEFFERSON *laughs.*)

SALLY: Tom's waitin'.

JEFFERSON: And I shan't disappoint him. Nor you.

(*He exits.* SALLY *picks up her cleaned corn and is about to exit when* PATSY *calls from offstage.*)

PATSY: Papa?! Papa?! (*She enters. She is about eight months pregnant.*)

SALLY: Why, Missy Patsy, what brings you all this way?

PATSY: Didn't Papa tell you?

SALLY: No'm. He must have forgot.

PATSY: Jeff wants to borrow a book. Where's Papa?

SALLY: At the naillery with Tom. Why don't you send Jeff down to join him? Them two boys love to raise Cain 'bout as much as we did.

PATSY: Don't be ridiculous. Tom was born to the naillery, not Jeff.

SALLY: Don't you be ridiculous, Miss Patsy.

(PATSY *starts off for the house.*)

SALLY: It's locked.

PATSY: The library?

SALLY: I've taken to lockin' it to protect your papa's privacy.

PATSY: But he's not even in there.

SALLY: It's still locked.

PATSY: Then open it. I want to get that book.

SALLY: He can get it for you when he gets back.

PATSY: Are you defying me, Sally?

SALLY: No'm. I'm just sayin' that since Mama died, the Master's put me in charge of runnin' the house, so I'm runnin' it. Same way you run Edgehill.

PATSY: It is not the same. Give me the key.

SALLY: (*Playing the dumb slave.*) I done forgotten where I left that key. But I'll hunt some more an' let you know jes' as soon's I finds it.

PATSY: Don't play dumb with me, Sally. I grew up with you, remember?

SALLY: Yes'm, I remember. Do you?

(JEFFERSON *enters.*)

JEFFERSON: Sally, the naillery is locked—Patsy, dearest!

PATSY: Hello, Papa.

(*They embrace warmly.*)

JEFFERSON: I forgot you were coming.

PATSY: So I see.

JEFFERSON: Did you bring Jeff?

PATSY: Yes. He wants to borrow a book, but it seems Sally has lost the key to the library.

JEFFERSON: Really?

SALLY: I think I know where to find it.

JEFFERSON: Good. Which book?

PATSY: Newton's *Principia*. Jeff has developed a passion for science.

JEFFERSON: Wonderful! I was quite interested in it myself at his age. Sally, fetch the *Principia* if you will.

SALLY: I cain't, Master.

JEFFERSON: Why not?

SALLY: You loaned it to Tom.

JEFFERSON: Oh, yes, I forgot. (*Proceeding carefully.*) Well, perhaps Jeff could start with another—

PATSY: (*Exploding*) Never mind, Papa! (*She starts off.*)

JEFFERSON: Patsy, come back here!

(PATSY *stops. She gets an idea and turns.*)

PATSY: Of course. As soon as Sally finds the key we'll go in and look for another book. If Sally'll let us.

JEFFERSON: Of course she will. Don't be ridiculous.

PATSY: I seem to have trouble avoiding that today. (*Beat*) By the way, Sally, when is your baby due?

SALLY: Feels like any minute now.

PATSY: You'll be suckling him, of course.

SALLY: Oh, yes, ma'am.

PATSY: Good. Then I'm sure you won't mind suckling mine. Your mama was the best mammy we had here at Monticello. I'm sure you'll make a good one, too.

SALLY: (*Tightly*) I'm not sucklin' your baby, Miss Patsy.

PATSY: Oh? Is that right, Papa?

(SALLY *turns quickly to* JEFFERSON.)

SALLY: Thomas?!

JEFFERSON: Patsy, must we discuss this now?

PATSY: Discuss it whenever you like, Papa. (*She exits.*)

SALLY: I am not sucklin' her child!

JEFFERSON: You promised you wouldn't fight with Patsy.

SALLY: An' you promised you wouldn't always take her side!

JEFFERSON: Sally—

SALLY: You even promised we'd go back to France. You won't see no mammies sucklin' in France, Thomas Jefferson!

JEFFERSON: We're in Virginia now, Sally.

SALLY: Don't I know it!

JEFFERSON: And I don't always take Patsy's side. But this time I have no choice.

SALLY: Why?

JEFFERSON: Because no one else is pregnant, no one else's milk will be flowing.

SALLY: *Hers* will! (*She starts off.*)

JEFFERSON: (*An imperious command*) Come back here!

(SALLY *freezes but does not turn around.* JEFFERSON *softens his tone.*)

JEFFERSON: Come back.

(SALLY *turns around.*)

JEFFERSON: Sally, Patsy won't do it and I can't make her.

SALLY: Why?

JEFFERSON: It's just not done. Good God, don't make this harder for me than it already is. Is it really so much to ask?

SALLY: It's everything! You take our sweat, our blood, an' now you want the milk from our bodies! Just how much you think we got to give?!

JEFFERSON: (*Going to her.*) Sally—

SALLY: Leave me alone! Go on, I want to be alone!

(JEFFERSON *reluctantly exits.* SALLY *begins pacing around the yard, muttering to herself.*)

SALLY: What's wrong with her titties, that's what I want to know. . . . She don't want to ruin 'em, is what. . . . How could you ruin those puny lil' peaks? . . . Her "Monticellos". . . . (*She laughs, despite herself.*) Oh, chile, I don't know. Maybe that's why the Lord done give me the Alps in the first place. . . . You on one breast, Patsy's on the other. . . . Well, maybe that'll bond you better than blood. Yeah, maybe y'all'll start out like me an' Miss Patsy—an' end better.

(PATSY *comes out on the porch. She and* SALLY *exchange a long, smoldering look. Suddenly* SALLY's *face transforms as she undergoes her first labor pain. She clutches her stomach and cries out.*)

PATSY: Sally! What is it?!

SALLY: The baby's comin', Missy, it's comin!

(SALLY *instinctively reaches out for* PATSY, *who hesitates the briefest moment, then runs to her. Their eyes meet for a brief moment in mutual understanding, then* PATSY *puts her arm around* SALLY *and begins helping her into the house as the lights change to . . .*)

Scene 2

(*The Front Porch and Yard. Late February, 1801. Morning on a crisp, beautiful day.* JEFFERSON *carries on a theodolite, sights, then calls to* TOM *offstage.*)

JEFFERSON: Higher! (*He sights again, calls.*) Higher still! (*Sights*) Hold it there.

(*He writes down the calculation.* SALLY *enters with a bundle of clothes and a boy's coat which she is sewing.*)

JEFFERSON: Now move five paces to your left. . . . I said your *left!*

SALLY: Calm down, Thomas. (*She places the clothes over the basket of corn, sits and sews.*)

JEFFERSON: If he's going to become an architect, he'd best learn his right from his left.

SALLY: It was a simple mistake. What's got you so riled up today?

JEFFERSON: I am not "riled up," I am simply trying to finish my house. (*Calls to* TOM.) Now complete your drawing for me! (*He goes back to his own drawings.*)

SALLY: I got a letter from James yesterday. He says the Revolution's finished an' it seems like a lot of blood spilled for nothin'. I wish he'd quit runnin' 'roun' Europe an' come back home where—

JEFFERSON: Damn!

SALLY: Now what?

JEFFERSON: I can't find a way of hiding the bedroom windows.

SALLY: Why would you want to?

JEFFERSON: To make my three-storied house seem to have only two.

SALLY: You mean like Madame du Barry's Pavillion de Louveciennes in Paris? 'Member how she had her bedroom windows on the floor level?

JEFFERSON: Sally, that's it! (*He sketches, excitedly.*) Yes ... Wonderful ...

SALLY: You sure you want folks to have to bend down every time they want to see out?!

JEFFERSON: Yes, I love clever disguises.

SALLY: I wonder if the people know they elected an architect instead of a president. (*She holds up the coat.*) There!

JEFFERSON: Is that for Tom?

SALLY: Uh-huh. For his trip to Washington.

JEFFERSON: Sally, are you mad? Tom can't go to Washington.

SALLY: I'll look after him.

JEFFERSON: You?!—

SALLY: I'll take care, Thomas. Nobody's gonna know who we are or where we came from.

JEFFERSON: Sally, if—

SALLY: There's no use huffin' an' puffin'. I'm not about to miss the biggest day in your life. I'm proud of you, Thomas, an' I want to be there. And don't worry, our love will be like your bedroom windows: impossible to see from without, impossible to forget from within.

(*She touches his cheek tenderly.* JEFFERSON *recoils in horror.*)

JEFFERSON: What are you doin?! Madison is here, and Patsy, Jeff—

SALLY: I forgot—

JEFFERSON: If this is an indication of the care you'll take—

SALLY: No one saw. Why are you so angry?

JEFFERSON: I am not angry!

SALLY: Coulda fooled me. Why is Master Madison here anyway? You'll be seein' him in Washington soon enough.

JEFFERSON: There are some important matters which need my immediate attention.

SALLY: (*Beat*) Will you write me?

JEFFERSON: It's dangerous, Sally—

SALLY: I know, but I need somethin' of you when you're not here. Please, Thomas.

JEFFERSON: You promise to destroy the letters, just like in France?

SALLY: Yes.

JEFFERSON: If I can get a letter safely to you I shall.

SALLY: Thank you, Thomas.

JEFFERSON: Sally, I need to talk to you. (*Proceeding carefully*) I am grossly in debt.

SALLY: That's nothin' new!

JEFFERSON: Let me finish—

(MADISON *calls from offstage.*)

MADISON: Mr. President? Are you there?

(*He enters, carrying several sheets of paper.* JEFFERSON *immediately disengages from* SALLY.)

JEFFERSON: And how was your walk?

MADISON: Fine. I took your draft with me, sat under one of your beautiful pines, and gave it a thorough going-over. Evenin', Sally.

SALLY: Evenin', Master Madison.

MADISON: Critta tells me you're expecting another child. Got a name yet?

SALLY: James has always been one of my favorites.

MADISON: Excellent choice! And if it's a girl?

SALLY: I was thinkin' 'bout Martha. 'Course I'd have to clear it with the father.

JEFFERSON: (*Quickly*) Sally, make sure Tom sets another place for dinner.

SALLY: Yes, Master. (*Flashing a glorious smile at* MADISON.) Welcome to Monticello! (*She exits with the basket of clothes.* MADISON *looks after her.*)

MADISON: That is a remarkably handsome woman. You're lucky to own her.

JEFFERSON: Yes . . .

MADISON: Well, shall we discuss your address? I think it a Magna Carta in politics.

JEFFERSON: Later. First I have a more pressing . . . need. (*Beat*) Mr. Madison, I have seriously miscalculated my ability to turn Monticello into a profitable plantation. My naillery is a failure, last spring's flooding cost me dearly. And the position of president pays abominably. No man will ever get rich on public office in this country. In short, my creditors are demanding their due, and I am unable to meet their demands without resorting to . . . unpleasant necessities.

MADISON: What necessities?

JEFFERSON: It is my fate to owe money and own slaves, both circumstances being contrary to my principles. Nevertheless, I must use the one to offset the other. I must sell some slaves.

MADISON: I see.

JEFFERSON: (*Ironically*) Naturally, as president of *all* the people, it would be ill-advised for me to do so publicly.

MADISON: Naturally.

JEFFERSON: Mr. Bacon has the list and knows my needs. (*Suddenly passionate*) Jemmy, if something is not done soon we shall be the murderers of our own children!

MADISON: Our own children? What do you mean?

JEFFERSON: *Rien.*

MADISON: I shall see that they are sold without your name being known.

JEFFERSON: Thank you, my friend.

MADISON: (*Beat*) I, too, have a pressing matter to discuss, Mr. President.

JEFFERSON: Yes?

MADISON: James Callendar approached me about being appointed postmaster at Richmond. And he hinted darkly that if you were so ungrateful as to overlook him now, he had certain facts in his possession he might no longer overlook in the future. Do you know what he means?

JEFFERSON: No.

MADISON: He says you sent him hush money.

JEFFERSON: I sent him fifty dollars as a reward! Such a misconstruction of my charities puts an end to them forever. Tell him the post is out of the question.

MADISON: It is a minor post, Thomas—

JEFFERSON: I will not go into the presidency with my hands tied. The answer is "no."

MADISON: Very well, Mr. President.

(Sally *enters.*)

Sally: Supper will be soon, Mr. Madison. Perhaps you would like to wash?

Madison: Thank you, Sally.

Jefferson: I'll accompany you.

Sally: May I speak to you for a moment, Master?

Jefferson: Now, Sally?

Sally: Yes!

Madison: I'll see you at table. (*He exits.*)

Jefferson: Sally, what's this all about? You know you mustn't—

Sally: It's about the "important matters" which needed your "immediate attention." Bacon let the word slip. The whole quarters is buzzin'. Why didn' you tell me?!

Jefferson: I didn't want to hurt you.

Sally: *Me*?! What about *them*?! You promised you'd never sell another slave.

Jefferson: I promised to try. I've sold all the land I can. I've mortgaged my slaves, my equipment, everything.

Sally: Even your beloved Monticello?

Jefferson: I must have a place to live.

Sally: Reasons, reasons, reasons! Those are my people! "Mistress Sal, she'll take care of us." "Yessuh, she keeps the keys now."

Jefferson: As President I shall do all in my power to abolish this abomination, but I cannot cure it by administering a massive dose of one of your mama's magic healing potions! Sally, I have the wolf by the ears and can neither hold him nor safely let go. Justice is in one scale, self-preservation in the other.

SALLY: An' how far will you go to preserve yourself, Thomas? Will you even sell me?

JEFFERSON: (*Goes to her.*) Sally, dearest—

SALLY: (*Taunting*) People might be watchin', Thomas.

JEFFERSON: (*Takes her arm.*) Come over here.

SALLY: (*Not moving*) Let go.

JEFFERSON: Sally, if you'll—

SALLY: Turn. Me. Loose!

(JEFFERSON *releases her. She turns, picks up* TOM'S *coat, throws it at his feet, then walks proudly off.* JEFFERSON *bends and picks up the coat as the lights change to . . .*)

Scene 3

(*By the banks of the Rivanna River. A few days later, late afternoon. The sound of gurgling water.* SALLY *is looking at the water as* JEFFERSON *joins her, weary and upset. There is a tenseness between them.*)

SALLY: Are they sold?

JEFFERSON: Yes.

SALLY: Did you have to break up any families?

JEFFERSON: No.

SALLY: I want Tom to go away. I don't want him growin' up aroun' this. Take him to Washington with you an' get him a job workin' with Benjamin Banneker. I want him to work for a black man he can respect.

JEFFERSON: All right, Sally.

SALLY: An' I want you to promise I can leave any time I want an' take my children with me.

JEFFERSON: Sally, you know I would never stop—

SALLY: Swear it!

JEFFERSON: I promise. (*Beat. He goes closer to the water's edge.*) This used to be my swimmin' hole. Once when I was ten a slave named Robert and I were playing "king of the cliff" on that embankment over there. Robert was big, probably didn't know his own strength, and he pushed me too hard and knocked me into the water. I cut my leg on that rock there and for some reason the sight of my own blood made me furious. I scrambled up the bank to Robert and struck him. Cut his lip. He just stared at me. "Come on, fight!" I yelled, and struck him again. "You the massa's son," he said. "If I hit you, he'll sell me." "No, he won't!" I screamed, knocked him down, and began to pummel him wildly, hitting and hitting. He warded off my blows, but he never struck back. Finally I rolled off him and lay in the sand, exhausted. Robert got up, soaked his shirt in the river, came back and stood over me and said, "Let's see 'bout your leg." (JEFFERSON *is quite emotional now.*) Lying in bed that night I began to tremble. There was something dark and evil inside that scared me. You see, Sally, once I knew Robert wouldn't fight back, I began to enjoy hitting him all the more. (*Beat.* JEFFERSON *is fighting back tears.*) I've never struck another slave. And I know the day I do, slavery has won. (*Beat*) You're the only person I've ever told that story.

(SALLY *goes to him and tenderly strokes his hair.* JEFFERSON *suddenly hugs her hard, out of his great need, and cries out.*)

JEFFERSON: Sally!

(*She cradles his head as the lights change to* ...)

Scene 4

(*The Study at Monticello. Night, late August, 1802. The sound of crickets.* SALLY *enters and begins reading as* JAMES *approaches the room, whistling* "Yankee Doodle." *He enters and watches* SALLY *for a moment. A sweater and knitting lie on a table.*)

JAMES: Evenin', Sally.

SALLY: James?! Oh, James, you've come back!

(*She embraces him.* JAMES *stands stiffly, trying to stifle his feelings.*)

SALLY: I was so afraid somethin' had happened to you. But now you're here! Oh, hug me, Brother, hug your Rabbit.

JAMES: (*Unable to hold back, he hugs her.*) Rabbit, Rabbit, Rabbit! Yes, I'm back. Did you think I'd leave you here forever? We're gonna be together again.

SALLY: Oh, yes, James. Come back to Monticello!

JAMES: (*Grabbing her shoulders and looking at her hard, then:*) Where does he keep his brandy?

SALLY: There ain't no—idn' any—in here.

JAMES: Oh, there *ain't, ain't* there? Well, I'll just drink the po' folks liquor, then. No use puttin' on airs. (*He takes out a flask and downs some liquor.*) Well, Sally, you look right at home here. Yessuh, a real little scene of domestic tranquillity, ain't that the phrase? (*Picking up the sweater.*) Who's this for, yours or Patsy's? I hear you been sucklin' white babies, Rabbit. Mama'd be real proud of you.

SALLY: I did what I had to do, James. Mama'd understand.

JAMES: Don't be too sure!

SALLY: If you came just to taunt me—

JAMES: I came to save you!

SALLY: I don't need savin'. He promised me my freedom whenever I asked.

JAMES: Show me the paper! 'Cause without it, a white man's promise will dry up like a parched persimmon.

SALLY: I don't need a piece of paper, James. An' the day I do is the day I got to leave.

JAMES: Sally, wake up! You're like that rabbit we trapped in the light, dazzled by it, cain't move a muscle—

SALLY: 'Cause I don't *wanna* move! Yes, I am in a light, a warm an' wonderful light. But it doesn' trap me, James, it frees. 'Cause when you're lookin' from the light, you cain't tell the color of whoever's holdin' that lantern. White, black—it just doesn't matter. All that matters is that you are in their light, an' it is brightenin' your whole soul.

JAMES: Still dreamin', ain't you, Rabbit? Well, one day maybe you'll have a dream that'll finally wake you up.

SALLY: (*Picks up the sweater.*) How many sweaters did you an' me have growin' up, James? (*Picks up a book.*) How many books did we read about the Greeks? (*Gestures to the whole room.*) This must be a dream, it has to be a dream. Every mornin' Sally Hemings wakes up in the President's bed. But I'm not dreamin', James. I am gettin' what I want.

JAMES: Yeah, you lookin' real plump, Miss Sally, with your fine grammar an' your clean dress. But be

careful, 'cause you know what they say: Fattenin'
hogs ain't in luck. They sure ain't. (*He laughs, then
suddenly begins singing to the tune of* "Yankee Doodle".)

Of all the damsels on the green,
On mountain, or in valley,
A lass so luscious ne'er was seen,
As Monticellian Sally—

SALLY: What's that song? Did you make it up? If you
did, it idn' funny.

JAMES: No, Rabbit, I heard folks singin' it in the
taverns down in Richmond. They thought it was funny, they thought it was real funny.

Yankee Doodle, who's the noodle?
What wife were so handy?
To breed a flock of slaves for stock,
A blackamoor's the dandy!

SALLY: Stop this, James—

JAMES: Come on, Sally, I know you love to sing. We
might even get ol' Tom to play along. He's gonna
have lots of time for fiddlin' soon, 'cause looks like
two years of presidentin's all he's gonna get. (*He
sings with ever-mounting intensity.*)

What though she by the glands secretes—

SALLY: James!—

(*She attempts to run from the room, but* JAMES *blocks
her way.*)

JAMES:
Must I stand shilly-shally?
Tuck'd up between a pair of sheets
There's no perfume like Sally.

SALLY: Please stop!

(*She attempts to cover her ears, but* JAMES *pulls away
her hands and keeps singing.*)

JAMES:
When pressed by loads of state affairs
I seek to sport an' dally—

SALLY: Don't—

JAMES:
The sweetest solace of my cares
Is in the *lap* of Sally.

Yankee doodle, who's the noodle?

SALLY: James!—

JAMES:
Wine's vapid, tope me brandy—
For still I find to breed my kind,
A NEGRO-WENCH THE DANDY!!!

(SALLY *collapses in tears.*)

SALLY: Please . . . please . . . no more . . . no . . . more
. . . no . . .

(JAMES *stands over his sister for a frozen moment,
then kneels to comfort her.*)

JAMES: Shh . . . shh . . . Sally, quiet now, quiet . . .
Your secret is out, Sister, that's why I came. But I'm
gonna take care of you, like I promised Mama. Just
as soon's we get off this mountain.

SALLY: Run away? . . .

JAMES: You think he wants you here when the
reporters come? You got to run now 'fore he finds
out an' sells you.

SALLY: Sells me?!

JAMES: Yes! His real mistress is politics, Rabbit! You
know it's true! When there's somethin' he knows he's
gotta do, does he care what *you* think? Does he even
bother to ask? (*Takes* Notes on Virginia *from his
pocket.*) Here's the real Thomas Jefferson, the one
who'll sell you quick as his lowest field hand to save
his "great an' noble" reputation.

SALLY: (*Fighting her doubts.*) He loves me!

JAMES: He loves owning you!

SALLY: No!

JAMES: Why are you stuck in the Tar Baby so strong?!

SALLY: I'm not stuck, I can leave whenever I want!

JAMES: But you *don't* want, do you?! If you left you'd have to claim your own life, but long as you're a slave you ain't got no worries. 'Cause you ain't got no choices. That's it, idn' it, Sally? Satan's done finally snatched you to his bosom: You actually like bein' owned!

SALLY: Get out!

(*She attempts to slap him, but* JAMES *grabs her wrist.*)

JAMES: Not without you. (*He drags her toward the door.*)

SALLY: Let go!

JAMES: Not till we're off this damn mountain forever!

SALLY: Stop! Thomas!

JAMES: You're gonna live free like we promised Mama!

SALLY: Turn me loose! Thomas!!!

(JEFFERSON *runs in.*)

JEFFERSON: What are you doing?!

(JAMES *whirls on him.*)

JEFFERSON: James!

JAMES: Well, lookee here, it's "Master President." Have you come to protect your property?

(SALLY *wrenches free and runs into* JEFFERSON'S *arms.*)

JAMES: Or is your property gonna protect you?

JEFFERSON: What do you want?

JAMES: I want my sister! (*He pulls out a knife.*)

SALLY: James!

JEFFERSON: Get out of the way, Sally.

SALLY: Thomas—

JEFFERSON: Do it!

(SALLY *moves away.*)

JEFFERSON: You won't kill me, James. I know you. I watched you grow up, remember, raised you with special care. And I know James Hemings could never kill another man, black . . . or white. Am I wrong? You're the master now, James. How will you treat your slave?

JAMES: You know, you know! Yeah, you always know, don't you, "Master." Well, maybe for once in his life Thomas Jefferson didn't know it all!

(JAMES *advances to strike* JEFFERSON, *knife in the air.* SALLY *screams and runs to* JAMES, *but* JEFFERSON *doesn't move.*)

SALLY: James, don't!

(JAMES *stops the knife, inches from* JEFFERSON. *A long beat.*)

JAMES: Naw . . . I'm gonna let your own kind do you in. (*Urgently*) Come with me, Sally! Cut that slavery snake from 'roun' your neck 'fore it strangles you to death!

(SALLY *shakes her head.*)

JAMES: Oh, Rabbit . . . Rabbit. . . . (*The life seems to drain from his body. He lets the knife fall to the floor. To* JEFFERSON:) I came lookin' for my sister, but I cain't seem to find her. Do me a favor, though: If you see her (*Looking right at* SALLY.) tell her I'm dead. (*He exits.*)

JEFFERSON: Are you all right?

(SALLY *nods.*)

JEFFERSON: I'd better make sure he leaves. I'll be right back, Sally.

(JEFFERSON *exits.* SALLY, *shaken, turns back into the room. She spies the copy of* Notes on Virginia *lying on the floor. She picks it up and opens it to begin reading as she slowly leaves the room, singing as she goes.*)

SALLY:
Slavery chain's done broke at last, broke at last, broke at last.
Slavery chain's done broke at last, gonna praise God till I die.

(*As* SALLY *sits in a corner of the stage and begins reading, the lights change to . . .*)

Scene 5

(*The Study. The next day.* MADISON *reads from a newspaper as* JEFFERSON *listens. Throughout the scene* SALLY *can be seen off to the side, in very dim light, reading* Notes on Virginia.)

MADISON: "It is well-known that the man, whom it delighteth the people to honor, for many years has kept, as his concubine, one of his slaves. Her name is Sally. The delicacy of this arrangement must strike every portion of common sensibility. By this mahogany-colored charmer our president has had several children—" Never have I read such damnable lies!

JEFFERSON: Did I really argue the virtues of a free press? The Creator surely has a deft touch with irony.

MADISON: Your levity is admirable under the circumstances, Mr. President. But November is only two months away. The Congressional elections—and your young presidency—hang in the balance. Callendar's accusations must be denounced as the insidious and vicious fabrications of a deranged mind!

JEFFERSON: And if they are not fabrications?

MADISON: No more joking, sir. With all due respect, I am weary of it.

(JEFFERSON *considers, then speaks directly to* MADISON.)

JEFFERSON: I, too, am weary, my friend. Weary of the tyranny of my secret.

(*Beat*)

MADISON: (*Shocked*) What are you saying?! A thing so foreign to your character?!

JEFFERSON: To lie with her? I am a man, Mr. Madison, like other men. There is nothing foreign to my character there. To keep her a slave, and our children, too? I would that *were* foreign to my character, for when I meet my Maker I shall have to face that great perversion of my soul. Yes, I have a slave mistress. It is at once my sin and my solace.

MADISON: I will not believe it.

JEFFERSON: It is true. Mr. Callendar only omitted to write that I believe I love her.

MADISON: Love her—? Thomas, how can you love something you own?

JEFFERSON: I don't know. But I want to believe I can, need to believe it, Jemmy. Perhaps here is an opportunity to prove that it's true.

MADISON: (*Incredulous*) You mean to admit these charges?

JEFFERSON: Why not?

MADISON: Because you will destroy in an instant all we have striven so mightily to attain.

JEFFERSON: (*Passionately*) No, slavery will destroy it! Hatred, bloodshed, undying prejudice, is that to be our legacy? Don't you see, all our ideals about freedom and equality are pointless posturings because we neglected to include the black man. Why not seize this moment and with one bold stroke open the door to our liberty and let him in? Why not say to our countrymen, "If this nation is to be possible, then Sally and I *must* be possible!?"

MADISON: Because they will revile you, repudiate you, and refuse to follow you. This is not the time!

JEFFERSON: (*Anguished*) Then when is?! I have lain with that harlot, politics, Jemmy, and am afflicted with her most dread disease: self-compromise. Am I to be remembered as the man who fathered the sacred sentiments of our freedom and then had not the courage to keep them alive? No! I must save my country.

MADISON: You will save it to death! (*Beat*) Why not free Sally?

JEFFERSON: You know the law: A freed slave must quit Virginia within the year. To free her is to lose her, and that I cannot do.

MADISON: Then do nothing!! (*Beat. He proceeds more calmly.*) Tom, it was you who taught me to attempt no more good than the nation can bear. You must be silent on this matter to the grave. Or its scandal will cast a shadow 'cross your life that will obscure forever the honor and reward that so deservedly are yours. If you admit these charges, you will lose the presidency, Sally—perhaps even your life. Find some other way to prove your love. Loving Sally Hemings may be your most bold and courageous act of all. Let that be enough, Tom, I beg of you.

JEFFERSON: I shall consider it.

MADISON: Good. (*Gets an idea, knowing how* PATSY *must feel.*) Let me send Patsy to you.

JEFFERSON: What for?

MADISON: You have nurtured her on the principles of kindness and understanding. Examine her heart. Let her feelings be your barometer. If she will stand beside you, then perhaps your countrymen will as well.

JEFFERSON: Very good. But I am confident of her support.

MADISON: Remember, Thomas: If you drop this stone it will ripple for a long, long time.

JEFFERSON: Send Patsy to me and I shall deal with the first wave.

(MADISON *turns to go.*)

JEFFERSON: Jemmy, try to understand.

MADISON: What is there to understand? (*With enormous sorrow at this realization.*) As you said, you are a man like other men.

(*He exits.* JEFFERSON *waits patiently for* PATSY, *scanning the newspaper. She enters.*)

JEFFERSON: You have heard the news?

PATSY: Yes, Papa, I'm so glad. Now we can end this sordid secrecy. Now we can be together again. We'll read, play music, take walks—all the things we did before Paris. Oh, Papa! (*Hugs him.*)

JEFFERSON: Patsy, dearest, it is so important for you to be with me when I take this bold step. Madison has told you I am going to admit the charges?

PATSY: What?!

JEFFERSON: Yes, and press forward to abolish slavery forever.

PATSY: You can't be serious?!

JEFFERSON: Quite serious. And we shall rely on our love to see us through the difficult time ahead.

PATSY: Your love was not something to be relied on, Papa, it was something to be earned. "The more you learn, the more I love you." So I learned: history, literature, music, painting, sculpture, French. I learned to dress well, talk well, spell well. I did everything I could to earn your love, Papa. But you gave it to Sally for free!

JEFFERSON: Patsy, child, I never realized—

PATSY: Because you're blind, Papa. Buildings, sculptures, ideas you see with a keen, keen eye, but you can't see people. You can't see that the Negro who serves you dinner resembles you more than the grandson who kisses your cheek. You can't see that the daughter who sits at your side can notice the thick, *black* hairs on your collar. I doubt, Papa, that you even see the woman you make love to every night.

JEFFERSON: Why are you saying this?

PATSY: Because of Mama! Remember when she died, Papa? I led you near insensible in here, where you curled up like a puppy in my lap and together we cried our great grief into that long, black night. For three weeks you'd pace and weep and pace again, till exhaustion gave you rest. You would have died, Papa, had I not forced you to horse. How we rode, ten hours at a stretch! Rambling through the woods, racing 'cross a sunlit field or bolting through the dark. Pounding, pounding over the earth till we had pounded our grief into the ground. (*She is weeping now.*) How you loved her, Papa! Oh, you loved my Mama so. Don't defile her now. Please . . . please . . . please. . . .

JEFFERSON: (*Comforting her.*) What would you have me do?

PATSY: (*Measuring her words.*) Sell Sally into Mississippi.

JEFFERSON: Patsy!

PATSY: Yes, Papa! Then when the reporters come there will be no evidence to contradict you. Then you can end your temptation forever. Then you can stand as tall as Thomas Jefferson once stood.

JEFFERSON: She is essential to me.

PATSY: To own, Papa, but not to love.

JEFFERSON: That is enough!

PATSY: Yes, Papa, it is. It is enough of Sally Hemings! Stop pretending, Papa. Remember, I share your soul. And when I look in it I see you'll never love Sally because of one simple fact: She's black.

JEFFERSON: Patsy—

PATSY: You hear me, Papa, black! And all your public declarations will never make her white!!

JEFFERSON: (*Exploding*) Enough!!! (*He regards* PATSY *for a long, hurt moment.*) Oh, Patsy, dearest child . . . How can you, of all people, speak so venomously of another of God's creatures? We will never talk of this again, never. Leave me now, I wish to be alone.

PATSY: Yes, Papa, alone. Where is Sally? She's not been seen all day. Perhaps she's heard the news and knows it's time to run. 'Cause she's afraid you'll be true to yourself and put her on the block!

(*On the word "block", the stage immediately goes to black except for a light on* SALLY, *who jerks her head up from her reading and stares straight ahead, horrified, as the lights change to . . .*)

Scene 6

(SALLY'S *nightmare. A public auction.* JAMES *enters,*

dressed as a plantation owner, carrying a small bench and a riding crop.)

JAMES: Nigger sale! Nigger sale! Gather ye round! (*To the audience*) Come on up here folks an' look what I got for y'all today. One of the finest niggers you ever laid eyes on, an' I'm gonna cry him off right here an' now. Nigger sale! Nigger sale!

(PATSY *and* LAFAYETTE (*and* MADISON) *enter.* SALLY *rises, keeping the book with her, and becomes part of the dream.*)

JAMES: Get on up there, Uncle.

(JAMES *cracks his crop against his boots, and* JEFFERSON *mounts the bench.*)

JAMES: Now, what am I bid for this fine nigger?

PATSY: One hundred thousand dollars!

JAMES: One hundred thousand dollars?! I get that for my puniest lil' pickaninnies. Look how tall this man is. An' strong, pick you a mess o' cotton. Let's hear me a decent bid.

SALLY: I love you.

(JAMES *ignores her.*)

PATSY: Fifty thousand dollars!

JAMES: (*Addressing* PATSY *intimately.*) Lookee here, I see you're a fine, 'spectable lady, you gonna 'preciate this nigger more in the house than in the fields. He's even-tempered: Tom, smile!

(*He cracks his crop and* JEFFERSON *smiles.*)

An' talented: Tom, play!

(*He cracks his crop and* JEFFERSON *mimes, playing* "Drink To Me Only With Thine Eyes" *on the violin while* SALLY *sings distortedly.*)

JAMES: An' smart: Uncle, say somethin' smart. (*He cracks his crop.*)

Jefferson: We hold these truths to be self-evident: That all men are created—

James: That's enough! You gotta watch him, he loves to hear hisself talk. He's a scientist, architect, inventor, lawyer, farmer, speaks three languages—this is a real Renaissance nigger! An' just look at that skin—almost pure white! I know how you ladies like your house boys to be light. You got to look deep to see the nigger in this man. It's in there, 'course— Lord knows there's a little nigger in us all. . . . (*To* Sally) Ain't that right?

Sally: I love you.

Patsy: One thousand dollars!

James: Now you're talkin'! (*He rips off* Jefferson's *shirt, exposing his chest. To* Patsy:) Go on, Missy, examine him. Examine him an' see if he suits you.

(Patsy *kisses* Jefferson *hard, sexually.* Sally *becomes agitated.*)

Patsy: One hundred dollars!

James: You see what I'm gettin' at now, don't you, Missy? This here nigger's gonna make you one fine, fine *breeder*!

(James *grabs* Jefferson's *groin and laughs.*)

Sally: Thomas!

James: (*To* Sally) I thought that particular part of his anatomy might interest you.

Sally: I love you.

James: Well, Tom, ain't you gonna answer the woman?

(Jefferson *remains silent.*)

Patsy: (*Satisfied*) One dollar.

James: (*To* Sally) So you wanna bid love, do you? Well listen up good, 'cause we're gonna hear from the only book this nigger ever wrote—an' I'll keep an ear cocked for any more love bids. (*Takes the book from* SALLY *and holds it up.*) *Notes on Virginia,* by Thomas Jefferson. In which we discover the differences between whites and blacks.

(PATSY, MADISON, *and* LAFAYETTE *recite from the book from memory. Their speech is hard, cold, and ugly, building in intensity like an oncoming train.* JAMES *throws in his asides quickly.*)

PATSY: "The first difference is that of color. Are not the fine mixtures of every passion in the one race preferable to that immovable veil of black which covers the emotions of the other."

JAMES: Darkies cain't blush!

LAYAFETTE: "In reason blacks are much inferior, as I think one could scarcely be found capable of comprehending the investigations of Euclid."

JAMES: Who be Euclid?

MADISON OR PATSY: "In imagination they are dull, tasteless, anomalous. Among blacks is misery enough, God knows, but no poetry."

JAMES: Niggers got no soul!

PATSY: They are more ardent after their female, but love seems with them more an eager desire than a tender, delicate mixture of sentiment and sensation.

JAMES: Niggers love fast!

PATSY/MADISON/LAYAFETTE: "They secrete less by the kidneys and more by the glands of the skin, which gives them a very strong and disagreeable odor."

JAMES: Niggers smell!

(JAMES *cracks his crop and all look to* JEFFERSON. *He looks appealingly to* JAMES, *who cracks his crop again, forcing* JEFFERSON *to speak. He does so, slowly and painfully.*)

JEFFERSON: "I have even noted that the orangutan shows a preference for . . .

(*He cannot continue, so* SALLY *finishes the quote, looking at* JEFFERSON.)

SALLY: ". . . Black women over those of his own species."

JAMES: APES PREFER NIGGER WOMEN!!! (*A long silence.* JAMES *hands* SALLY *the book.*) Now what do I hear from love? (*Silence*) Goin' once . . . (*Silence*) Goin' twice . . . (*Silence*) Goin' . . . Goin' . . . Gone! Sold to the white folks for . . . one soul.

(PATSY *leads* JEFFERSON *off,* LAFAYETTE *and* MADISON *exiting as well.* JAMES *raises his crop high in the air, then brings it down hard. On the sound, the lights black out on the rest of the stage, leaving* SALLY *in a pool of light. As she sings, she begins transforming herself from the master's mistress in her fine clothes and flowing hair into a simple darkey in a plain bandanna and soiled clothing.*)

SALLY:
There is a balm in Gilead to make the wounded whole.
There is a balm in Gilead to heal the sinsick soul.
There is a balm in Gilead to make the wounded whole.
There is a balm in Gilead to heal the sinsick soul.

Sometimes I feel discouraged and think my work in vain,
But then the Holy Spirit revives my soul again.

There is a balm in Gilead to make the wounded whole.
There is a balm in Gilead to heal the sinsick soul.
There is a balm in Gilead to make the wounded whole.
There is a balm in Gilead to heal the sinsick soul.

(SALLY *sings only enough of the song to complete her transformation, pick up a basin and towel, and move toward the Study as the lights change to . . .*)

Scene 7

(*The Study. The next morning.* JEFFERSON *stares anxiously out the window, perhaps scanning the horizon through his telescope. After a moment,* SALLY *enters, humming.*)

JEFFERSON: Sally, where have you been all night?

SALLY: Sittin' up in an ol' oak tree, lookin' at the sky, full of stars. Mama's ridin' one of them stars. Gonna be watchin' over me while I walk my rocky road.

JEFFERSON: I couldn't sleep. I was afraid you had . . . (*Doesn't want to say it.*)

SALLY: Run away? No, I'd never run away, Master. (*He is surprised by her use of "Master" in private.*)

JEFFERSON: Have you heard the news?

SALLY: Yes. I've come to bathe you. Figured your head must be troubled. (*She begins to bathe his head.*)

JEFFERSON: Thank you, Sally. And then we must decide what to do.

SALLY: *We*, Master?

JEFFERSON: Why do you keep calling me that? We're alone.

SALLY: I won't ever call you that again.

JEFFERSON: Still using your soap that makes you smell of smoldering fires. I have always loved your smell, Sally.

SALLY: Have you?

JEFFERSON: Hmmmm. You've always known just where to press.

(*She presses too hard.*)

JEFFERSON: Gently.

SALLY: Sorry, but you were the one who taught me the benefits of pain. When you vaccinated me.

JEFFERSON: It worked. We didn't catch smallpox.

SALLY: No, it ain't smallpox we caught, is it?

JEFFERSON: You haven't said "ain't" in a long time.

SALLY: No, I ain't. Well, I got to clean up this room. (*She gets a broom and begins sweeping.*)

JEFFERSON: How dark you are this morning.

SALLY: Yes, I feel a lot darker than I have in some time. But I'm surprised you could see it through my immovable veil of black.

JEFFERSON: What are you saying—Will you stop sweeping?!

SALLY: I got to sweep. "Clean up your own mess," ain't that what you always taught us? An' I done made a heap of mess in this room.

JEFFERSON: Sally! (*He grabs the broom and casts it aside.*) What's wrong with you?

SALLY: (*Handing him* Notes on Virginia.) What's wrong with you, Thomas?

JEFFERSON: You read this?

SALLY: How could you say such things? How could you?!

JEFFERSON: Sally, I wrote this twenty years ago. Before you. Before so much. Living with you has shown me the awful errors of my easy prejudice and I abhor it with all my heart. Oh, Sally, don't remember what I've writ but what I've lived.

SALLY: You've lived a lie. An' so have I.

JEFFERSON: And what is the truth?

SALLY: That you are capable of sellin' me.

JEFFERSON: Never!

SALLY: Yes. If you can think of no other way out of this scandal, you will sell me. You can do it. You own me!

JEFFERSON: Sally—

SALLY: You own me! This flesh an' blood an' lips an' eyes, you own it!

JEFFERSON: And you think that pleases me?

SALLY: Yes.

JEFFERSON: That I enjoy holding you one moment and having you fetch for me the next?

SALLY: Yes.

JEFFERSON: That I thrill to the sound of "Master" from your lips?!

SALLY: Yes, yes, yes! You know you do!

JEFFERSON: I don't!

SALLY: (*With an increasingly ugly sexuality*) When you take me in your arms an' peel off my fine silk Parisian nightgown an' I stand there tremblin' an' erect—

JEFFERSON: Sally—

SALLY: An' you bury your mouth in my coarse black hair an' inhale my dark an' dusky smell—

JEFFERSON: Why are you doing—?

SALLY: An' you penetrate, hard an' deep, an' tight—

JEFFERSON: Stop!—

SALLY: An' burst through me, fillin' me up with your white river, cryin' out "Sally! Sally! Sally!"—

JEFFERSON: I order you to stop!—

SALLY: Dusky Sally! Sable Sal! The Mahogany-Colored Charmer! You own me an' it pleasures you *all the more*!!!

(JEFFERSON *strikes her with the broom, knocking her down. A long pause, then quietly:*)

JEFFERSON: God-damn your soul to everlasting hell, Sally Hemings. (*Beat. Defeatedly.*) How can I free my country when I cannot even free myself? Lafayette was right: I am seduced.

SALLY: Well, I'm not, Thomas. No more, no more. I want my freedom an' the freedom of my children. Now. An' in writin'.

JEFFERSON: You'll be banished from the state.

SALLY: No, Thomas. Not if you file a formal petition with the legislature. Then I can stay.

JEFFERSON: That would be tantamount to admitting the truth!

SALLY: Yes! "An' the truth shall make you free." We'll both be free—an' equal.

JEFFERSON: I can't, Sally. The nation isn't ready!

SALLY: I am! I will let you master me no more. Now write me out my freedom like you promised.

(JEFFERSON *writes her manumission paper.*)

JEFFERSON: If you must go, always know that I have cared for you as I have no other. And always will. I love you, Sally. And here is the proof. (*He hands her the paper.*) I have let go the wolf's ears, Sally. Devour me if you will.

(JEFFERSON *turns away while* SALLY *reads the paper. A long beat. She holds the paper to her breast ... then slowly tears it up. Hearing the sound,* JEFFERSON *looks up.*)

SALLY: Silence has its virtues, Thomas.

(JEFFERSON *and* SALLY *exchange a long look. Then he takes the broom, places it at his feet, and holds out his hand to* SALLY. *She takes it, they slowly bend, and then jump over the broom as the lights change to ...*)

Scene 8

(*An open grave. July 4, 1826. Late afternoon. Darkening clouds. A* SLAVE *sings as he shovels dirt into the grave.*)

SLAVE:
When you face that judgment mawnin',
You got to face it by yo'sef
No one heah to face it faw you,
You got to face it by yo'sef.

(PATSY *enters, nods to the* SLAVE, *and he stands silently off to the side. She kneels over the grave.*)

PATSY: Well, Papa, you made it. You died on July 4th, on the fiftieth anniversary of your famous Declaration. Just like you wanted. Always in control, even of the hour of your death. And now you're back where you belong: next to Mama.

(SALLY *enters, unnoticed.*)

PATSY: She's been waiting for you, Papa, waiting all these years to ask you one question: Why? Why? Why? Why?

SALLY: You don't think he'll answer her, do you? He never was much good at explainin' himself, I don't guess he's gonna start now.

PATSY: What are you doing here?

SALLY: I got a right to be here, Missy. Let's don't start up. Not here. Not now. Let your papa rest in peace.

(PATSY *gives way.* SALLY *approaches the grave.*)

PATSY: You heard the will?

SALLY: Yes'm.

PATSY: $107,000 in debt. His legacy to me.

SALLY: Well, at least he finished his house.

Patsy: It will have to be sold. (*Beat*) Are you surprised he didn't do it, Sally?

Sally: Free me in his will? Leave you to do it instead after a "reasonable time?" No'm, I'm not surprised. I reckon I learned a few things from thirty-seven years of livin' with this man.

Patsy: But now there's nothing to tie you to him. People will never know.

Sally: Oh, folks'll find out one day, Missy. An' when they do, I hope they'll be glad. He would like that.

Patsy: Then why didn't he scratch in your name?

Sally: Well, Missy, maybe he needed to own me even in death. An' truth to tell, maybe there was even a part of me that needed to be owned.

Patsy: Is that why you stayed?

Sally: Freedom ain't the onliest dream, Miss Patsy. I stayed because I had found somethin' nobody can own: love. That was my freedom.

Patsy: And your slavery.

Sally: I reckon that's what love is, ain't it, Missy? Freedom an' slavery both.

Patsy: (*Considering the grave.*) He made me promise not to mourn him too much. Said he'd had a good life, done more than he'd ever dreamed. He told me, "Patsy, remember: The earth belongs to the living ..." (*She breaks into tears and falls into* Sally's *arms.*) Oh, Sally, I shall miss him so!

Sally: He loved you, Miss Patsy. He loved you so very much.

(*They hold each other. After a moment,* Patsy *straightens and hands* Sally *a clothbound package.*)

Patsy: From Papa. He said it was his legacy to you.

(PATSY *exits.* SALLY *lays the package aside and kneels over the grave.*)

SALLY: You know what I've been doin' all day, Thomas? Thinkin'. Tryin' to name all the flowers at Monticello. I got as far as forget-me-nots. Then I tried to remember all my French, every verb, every syllable. I got as far as ... "*Tu.*" (*She is fighting back tears.*) You see, it's not workin', Thomas. The head ain't stronger than the heart, like you said. You hear me?! (*Cries out to him angrily, perhaps throwing dirt on his coffin.*) It ain't! It ain't! It ain't! (*She breaks into sobs.*) Oh, Thomas, what you doin' down there an' me up here? . . . (*A long pause while* SALLY *regains control. The she pulls out a packet of letters.*) Here're the letters. From France, Philadelphia, Washington. Your words, your beautiful, beautiful words. (*Suddenly urgent*) Thomas, they're all I have left, why do I have to—? (*She hugs them fiercely to her bosom. Then, resignedly:*) I'know. 'Cause I promised. Just like you. (*She kisses the letters and lays them tenderly in the grave. Then she opens the package. It is a red ear of corn.* SALLY *is terribly moved.*) Oh, Thomas, can you hear me? I love you, too. (*The distant rumble of thunder.* SALLY *rises and looks at the sky.*) That you rumblin' 'roun' up there, Thomas Jefferson? Well, I got a superstition for you. When it rains on a fresh grave, you're sure to go to heaven. You hear that, Thomas? You are sure to go to heaven. I will see you there.

(SALLY *nods to the* SLAVE. *As he crosses in to finish his work, their eyes meet in a look of equality and mutual respect. The* SLAVE *seems to draw strength from* SALLY. *She exits and he begins shovelling in the dirt, singing.*)

SLAVE:
Oh, you got tuh walk-a that lonesome Valley
You got tuh go tha by yo'sef,
No one heah tuh go tha with you,
You got tuh go tha by yo'sef

(*The lights slowly dim out.*)

Finis

SET

Jefferson's Drawing Room, Hotel de Langeac, Paris
A desk and chair, an arm chair, a bookshelf stuffed with books, a telescope looking out through high French windows, perhaps a painting, a small stool for SALLY for the bathing

Patsy's Room
An elegant chair, perhaps a clothestand, and a full-length mirror (can be mimed)

The Ballroom
A chandelier and candelabra on stands

The Porch and Yard at Monticello
A high-backed rocking chair, a pillar or two, debris—bricks, nails, lumber—that suggest the house's being in a constant state of repair, and a standing writing table

Jefferson's Study at Monticello
A lounge chair, bookshelf, windows, a telescope, and a desk (or the writing table)

The Bois de Boulogne, Sally's Room, The Banks of the Rivanna River, The Slave Auction, and Jefferson's Open Grave*
These areas are defined by lighting, with perhaps the suggestions of trees and a mound of dirt for the grave.

---

*If desired, it is also possible to create a "Courtyard" for the last scene, and perhaps even the last two scenes, of Act One.